The Campus History Series

GEORGETOWN
UNIVERSITY

Surrounded by farmland, the Georgetown campus appears in the distance in this c. 1831 painting. Although it was the nation's capital, Washington remained a small town with few major improvements; a place that Charles Dickens described in 1842 as a city with "spacious avenues, that begin in nothing, and lead nowhere." That changed dramatically after the Civil War when the federal government expanded, streets were paved, sewers installed, and landmarks like the Capitol dome and Washington Monument were completed. (Georgetown University Booth Family Center for Special Collections.)

FRONT COVER: Construction of Healy Hall was completed 20 years before this c. 1900 photograph. Described as Patrick F. Healy, SJ's, far-flung gesture of confidence and resolve about Georgetown's future, Healy Hall is the iconic emblem of Georgetown University. (Georgetown University Booth Family Center for Special Collections.)

COVER BACKGROUND: Georgetown football players pose in front of Healy Hall around 1900. A football association began at Georgetown in 1874; the first team was formed in 1883. (Georgetown University Booth Family Center for Special Collections.)

The Campus History Series

GEORGETOWN

UNIVERSITY

Paul R. O'Neill and Bennie L. Smith

ARCADIA
PUBLISHING

Published by Arcadia Publishing
Charleston, South Carolina

Printed in the United States of America

Library of Congress Control Number: 2019954205

For all general information, please contact Arcadia Publishing:
Telephone 843-853-2070
Fax 843-853-0044
E-mail sales@arcadiapublishing.com
For customer service and orders:
Toll-Free 1-888-313-2665

Visit us on the Internet at www.arcadiapublishing.com

This book is dedicated to the women and men who, for more than 200 years, have been a part of Georgetown University's academic community in the Jesuit tradition of creating and communicating knowledge and living in service to others.

CONTENTS

ACKNOWLEDGMENTS

Those who have studied the history of Georgetown University know the indispensable resource, Dr. Emmett Curran's three-volume *A History of Georgetown University*. Dr. Curran's books provide a definitive understanding of the university from its founding to the modern era. The authors of this book relied heavily on Dr. Curran's research and scholarship, and we are deeply grateful to him.

The authors could not have completed this book without the expertise and guidance of university archivist Lynn Conway and assistant archivist Ann Galloway. Prof. John Glavin, PhD (C'64), an expert in Georgetown architecture and history, shared essential feedback. Content, structure, and flow were thoroughly reviewed by Deirdre Kenny (C'86). Feedback and edits were provided by Gregory Annick (C'86), Deborah Cunningham, Caroline Knickerbocker (S'15), and Judy Pezza Rasetti (G'97). Unless otherwise noted, the images in this book are from Georgetown University's Booth Family Center for Special Collections.

A letter and date follow the names of alumni to designate the Georgetown school they attended and their year of graduation:

B	McDonough School of Business
C	Georgetown College
F	School of Foreign Service
G	Graduate School
I	Institute of Languages and Linguistics
L	Law Center
LLM	Master of Laws
M	Medical School
N	School of Nursing and Health Studies
S	School of Continuing Studies

INTRODUCTION

"We shall begin the building of our Academy this summer," wrote John Carroll, SJ, in March 1788, referring to the construction of Old South, the first campus building of Georgetown University, the oldest Catholic and Jesuit university in the United States.

Georgetown University marks 1789 as the year of its founding. But few know that a mid-19th-century typographical error factors centrally in the history of Georgetown's founding date. Historian Emmett Curran discovered that for more than 50 years, Georgetown linked its beginning to 1788, the year that construction began on the first campus building, Old South. However, the 1851 college catalog incorrectly listed 1789 as the year that construction began. The 1873 catalog repeated the dating error and added another, stating for the first time that Georgetown was "founded as a College in 1789." The discrepancy was discovered some time after the university celebrated its centennial in 1889. So, when the error came to light, why didn't the university return to 1788 as the founding year—the year originally cited, the year the first building was started? Likely, university leaders were reluctant to compromise the romantic association with 1789, the year of George Washington's inauguration and the year the first US Congress met under the new Constitution. After all, they reasoned, 1789 was the year that John Carroll obtained the deed for the first parcel of campus land.

Founding a college in late-18th-century America was not an unusual undertaking. As Curran chronicled in *A History of Georgetown University*, 23 American colleges began between 1782 and 1800. What was unusual about Carroll's venture was that he was establishing a school without the guarantee of church or state funding, or the benefit of a private endowment.

Carroll's vision for Georgetown anticipated the importance of endowments. He believed that Catholic laity would provide considerable subscriptions in support of his venture. In his "Proposals for Establishing an Academy at George Town, Patowmack-River, Maryland" dated November 1786, Carroll outlined the purpose of the new school, writing that a "system [would] be effectually carried into existence" that would eliminate or substantially reduce the need to charge tuition to run the school.

Carroll sent copies of his Proposals with a one-page solicitation to elite Catholics in the United States and Europe. The solicitation was addressed "To all liberally inclined to support the education of youth" and asked for "generous donations for the purposes set forth" in the Proposals. In fact, Carroll received no substantial pledges of financial support for the new school, either in response to his initial outreach or the several campaigns that followed. As historian Joseph T. Durkin, SJ, put it: "Georgetown committed herself to becoming a university on a total average income (from all sources) of less than $150,000 a year."

The absence of a founding endowment would have lasting effect. "Georgetown's financial concerns," wrote the editor of *Georgetown* magazine in 1982, "are older than the University itself, and capital, or lack of it, is inextricably linked to the events that form the history of [Georgetown University]."

Despite an inextricable link with insufficient capital, Georgetown rose to national and international prominence in higher education. Its success can be attributed in part to the leadership of several visionary men, referred to in their day as Georgetown's "founders," who built on Carroll's original vision. Patrick F. Healy, SJ, president from 1873 to 1882, is universally considered to be Georgetown's "second founder." Timothy S. Healy, SJ, president from 1976 to 1989, is referred to in modern times as Georgetown's "third founder." Between the two Healys there were other consequential presidents—W. Coleman Nevils, SJ, for example, and Edward Bunn, SJ, who were each referred to historically as a Georgetown "founder." Inspired by the leadership and impact of these men, the content of this book is ordered around their tenure as presidents.

Georgetown University is not a comprehensive historical study, as space limitations dictate how broadly—or narrowly—the authors were able to address many topics. The selection of portraits, documents, and photographs reveals the authors' interest in the school's architecture; that is, history as bricks and mortar. Indeed, many of the images housed in the university archives, District of Columbia libraries, and the Library of Congress focus on the physical development of the campus. But also included are pictures and stories of Georgetown's community of leaders, faculty, students, alumni, and benefactors. On balance, the authors hope, the result is a varied and engaging look into Georgetown's first 200 years.

One

FOUNDING AND EARLY YEARS

In the early years, especially its first decade, Georgetown struggled to become viable. There were five presidents in the first 10 years, enrollment climbed and dropped unpredictably, and buildings were left unfinished for lack of funds. In 1806, John Carroll suggested in a letter to Pres. Robert Molyneux, SJ, that operations of the college be suspended. As Emmett Curran has commented, "It was scarcely an auspicious start."

Georgetown began to find its footing in its third decade under the leadership of Pres. John Grassi, SJ. During Grassi's presidency, in August 1814, the Society of Jesus was restored after 41 years of suppression. The restoration of the society provided Grassi with Jesuit faculty from Europe, who added numbers and intellectual depth to the college. In March 1815, Georgetown received a federal charter to grant academic degrees. As Curran wrote about Grassi's tenure, "Georgetown was becoming [at Carroll's death in 1815] the national college that Carroll had envisioned a generation earlier, open to students of every religion and class" and "the major domestic producer of clergy for his [the Catholic] church."

A burst in enrollment and a major building campaign under Pres. Thomas Mulledy, SJ, in the 1830s increased the prestige of the college further but left the school badly in debt. The sale in 1838 of 272 enslaved persons owned by the Jesuit province marked a dark chapter in Georgetown's history, as proceeds from the sale were used, in part, to pay down the college's debt.

Mulledy was part of what Curran described as the "Irish Troika," which included Mulledy, Pres. William McSherry, SJ, and Pres. James Ryder, SJ, each of whom was a Jesuit novice at the same time in Rome and returned to America with ambitious plans for Georgetown. When the President and Directors of Georgetown College was incorporated by Congress in 1844, Georgetown was the oldest and most prosperous of the 31 Catholic colleges in the United States.

This painting by John Moll depicts the *Ark* and the *Dove*, the two ships that in 1634 carried the first English settlers to the Maryland colony. Founded by Sir George Calvert, the first Lord Baltimore, the Maryland colony was unique at the beginning for permitting the free practice of Catholicism. Later in the 17th century, however, penal laws in Maryland prohibited Catholics from voting, worshipping publicly, or holding public office. These restrictions remained until the US Constitution guaranteed freedom of religion. (Courtesy of the Maryland Historical Society.)

The Settlement of Maryland by Lord Baltimore was painted in 1884 by Emanuel Gottlieb Leutze. The first English settlers in Maryland included Fr. Andrew White, SJ (standing left), accompanied by Fr. John Gravenor, SJ, and Brother Thomas Gervase, SJ, who came to minister to Catholic colonists and convert the native population. Despite British penal laws restricting the establishment of Catholic schools, the Jesuits operated covert schools for short periods. These early schools included one at Bohemia Manor on the eastern shore of the Chesapeake Bay, where John Carroll studied as a boy. (Courtesy of the Maryland Historical Society.)

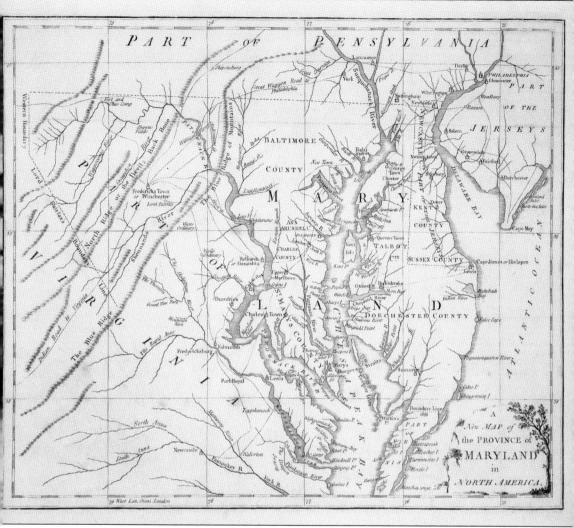

Upon the arrival of the first Jesuits in Maryland in 1634, a Jesuit mission was established. Like lay settlers, Jesuit priests arriving from England received land grants from the Maryland lord proprietor under the headright system. By the turn of the 18th century, the Jesuit settlers collectively had amassed several large plantations. Estimates by Emmett Curran put the Jesuits' landholdings at more than 12,000 acres. Proceeds from the plantations were a source of financial support for the Jesuit mission and also eventually for Georgetown University. First worked by indentured servants, by 1700, the plantations relied on the labor of enslaved people. Georgetown's 2015 Working Group on Slavery, Memory and Reconciliation documented the link between Georgetown's origins and growth to the profits of the Jesuit-owned and -operated plantations in Maryland. (Courtesy of the Maryland Historical Society.)

This portrait of Archbishop John Carroll, SJ, founder of Georgetown University, was completed by renowned portrait artist Gilbert Stuart around 1804. Carroll was born in 1735 to Daniel, an Irish immigrant, and Eleanor Darnall, Daniel's distant cousin and a wealthy heiress. Because Catholic education was illegal in Maryland at the time, Carroll attended a covert Jesuit school at Bohemia Manor in Maryland until 1748, when he was sent for further studies at the Jesuit College of St. Omers in French Flanders. Carroll entered the Society of Jesus in 1753 in the Netherlands and was ordained in 1761. The suppression of the Jesuits in 1773 prompted Carroll to return to Maryland, where the American Revolution was underway. Carroll himself was not substantially involved in the Revolution, but the Carroll family was well represented. His cousin Charles Carroll, notably, was the only Catholic signer of the Declaration of Independence, and his brother Daniel served in the first US Congress. For his part, John Carroll emerged as the leader of the 24 Catholic priests in America. When the Catholic Church established the first diocese in America in 1789, Carroll was appointed its first bishop. As bishop of Baltimore, Carroll assumed the burden of providing clergy for the church. He believed that a school was essential to offer "intellectual and moral training" for young men who could become priests.

PROPOSALS

FOR ESTABLISHING AN

ACADEMY,

AT GEORGE-TOWN, PATOWMACK-RIVER, MARYLAND.

THE Object of the proposed Institution is, to unite the Means of communicating Science with an effectual Provision for guarding and improving the Morals of YOUTH. With this View, the SEMINARY will be superintended by those, who, having had Experience in similar Institutions, know that an undivided Attention may be given to the Cultivation of Virtue, and literary Improvement; and that a System of Discipline may be introduced and preserved, incompatible with Indolence and Inattention in the Professor, or with incorrigible Habits of Immorality in the Student.

The Benefit of this Establishment should be as general as the Attainment of its Object is desirable. It will, therefore, receive Pupils as soon as they have learned the first Elements of Letters, and will conduct them, through the several Branches of classical Learning, to that Stage of Education, from which they may proceed, with Advantage, to the Study of the higher Sciences, in the University of this, or those of the neighbouring States. Thus it will be calculated for every Class of Citizens—as READING, WRITING, ARITHMETIC, the easier Branches of the MATHEMATICS, and the GRAMMAR of our NATIVE TONGUE will be attended to, no less than the LEARNED LANGUAGES.

Agreeably to the liberal Principle of our Constitution, the SEMINARY will be open to Students of EVERY RELIGIOUS PROFESSION.—They, who in this Respect differ from the SUPERINTENDENTS of the ACADEMY, will be at Liberty to frequent the Places of Worship and Instruction appointed by their Parents; but, with Respect to their moral Conduct, all must be subject to general and uniform Discipline.

In the Choice of Situation, Salubrity of Air, Convenience of Communication, and Cheapness of living, have been principally consulted; and GEORGE-TOWN offers these united Advantages.

The Price of Tuition will be moderate; in the Course of a few Years, it will be reduced still lower, if the System, formed for this SEMINARY, be effectually carried into Execution.

Such a Plan of Education solicits, and, it is not Presumption to add, deserves public Encouragement.

The following Gentlemen, and others, that may be appointed hereafter, will receive Subscriptions, and inform the Subscribers, to whom, and in what Proportion, Payments are to be made :—In Maryland—The Hon. CHARLES CARROLL, of CARROLLTON, HENRY ROZER, NOTLEY YOUNG, ROBERT DARNALL, GEORGE DIGGES, EDMUND PLOWDEN, Esqrs, Mr. JOSEPH MILLARD, Capt. JOHN LANCASTER, Mr. BAKER BROOKE, CHANDLER BRENT, Esq; Mr. BERNARD O'NEILL and Mr. MARSHAM WARING, Merchants, JOHN DARNALL, and IGNATIUS WHEELER, Esqrs, on the Western-Shore; and on the Eastern, Rev. Mr. JOSEPH MOSLEY, JOHN BLAKE, FRANCIS HALL, CHARLES BLAKE, WILLIAM MATTHEWS, and JOHN TUITTE, Esqrs.—In Pennsylvania—GEORGE MEAD and THOMAS FITZSIMMONS, Esqrs, Mr. JOSEPH CAUFFMAN, Mr. MARK WILCOX, and Mr. THOMAS LILLY.—In Virginia—Col. FITZGERALD, and GEORGE BRENT, Esq;—and at New-York, DOMINIC LYNCH, Esquire.

SUBSCRIPTIONS will also be received, and every necessary Information given, by the following Gentlemen, Directors of the Undertaking :—The Rev. Messrs. JOHN CARROLL, JAMES PELLENTZ, ROBERT MOLYNEUX, JOHN ASHTON, and LEONARD NEALE.

"Proposals for Establishing an Academy at George Town, Patowmack-River, Maryland," dated November 1786, is the earliest printed document relating to Georgetown's founding. It describes Carroll's plan to establish a school open to "students of every religious profession" and "every class of citizens." Aligned with the academy's academic mission were strict provisions for "guarding and improving the morals of youth," as well as the "cultivation of virtue." Although the word "Catholic" does not appear anywhere in the document, printed copies of the Proposals were broadly distributed among Catholic elites in America and abroad whom Carroll hoped would fund his new venture.

To all liberally inclined to promote the Education
of YOUTH.

BE it known by thefe prefents, that I, the underwritten, have ~~appointed~~ *humbly requested* *Edw.? Weld Esq.r & Lady*

to receive any generous donations for the purpofes

fet forth in a certain printed paper, entitled,

Proposals for eftablifhing an Academy, at George-Town,
Patowmack-River, Maryland;

for which *they* will give receipts to the benefactors, and remit the monies received by *them* to me

the aforefaid underwritten, one of the directors of this undertaking.

Confcious alfo of the merited confidence placed in the aforefaid *Edward Weld Esq.r & Lady*

defire
I moreover ~~authorize~~ *them* to appoint any other perfon or perfons to execute the fame liberal office, as

they *are humbly requested* ~~is authorized~~ by me to execute.

~~Given at~~ *Maryland*, this *30th* day of *March* 17 *87*

Signed and fealed

J. Carroll

Carroll's letter initiating fundraising for his proposed school, dated March 1787, was sent to prospective donors along with his Proposals. Without the benefit of state sponsorship or private endowment, Carroll relied on revenue from student tuition, the labor of enslaved persons on Jesuit-owned plantations, and periodic but typically small bequests from individuals. Carroll's dogged determination to open the school without an endowment created a condition that plagued the school, almost fatally, for much of its first century.

This is the campus as it appeared in 1792 when Georgetown's first classes were held in Old South, a small Georgian-style redbrick structure with a commanding view of the Potomac River. Construction of Old South began in April 1788 and took three years to complete because of regular shortfalls in money to pay for materials and laborers. Old South stood for more than 100 years before it was demolished and replaced by Ryan Hall.

Since the mid-1800s, Georgetown's founding has been tied to the date of this deed, January 23, 1789, when John Carroll acquired the title to a one-acre plot of farmland where Old South was already under construction. Carroll's selection of this hilltop property was influenced by many factors, including the "salubrity of air" and "cheapness of living," as mentioned in the Proposals. Unbeknownst to Carroll, however, the location would become significant when the Residence Act of 1790 located the District of Columbia nearby and forever tied Georgetown's history with that of the nation's capital.

Robert Plunkett, SJ (1791–1793), was the first president of Georgetown. Recruiting someone to serve as president proved an onerous task for John Carroll, and many of his preferred candidates declined his entreaties to serve. Plunkett took the job but served for only 18 months. When it opened, the "Academy" comprised three divisions: elementary, preparatory, and college. Georgetown was more geographically diverse than other American schools at the time, a trend influenced by Bishop Carroll's pastoral letter to American Catholics asking that they send their sons to Georgetown. Faculty and students drawn from up and down the East Coast of the new nation and from abroad gave Georgetown a national and international character that distinguished it from other schools at the time.

Modeled after Nassau Hall at Princeton University, construction of Old North (the oldest academic building on campus) began in 1794 after John Carroll purchased two acres of farmland to enlarge the campus. By Georgetown standards at the time, Old North was massive—almost three times longer than Old South and four stories tall. The "North Building" would provide dormitory space, classrooms, and a student chapel, but as with Old South, a lack of funds caused construction delays. The exterior of the building was substantially complete in 1795, but it was not opened until 1797, and the interior was not fully finished until 1809.

Washington addressing the Student
from the porch of
"Old North"
1796

In August 1797, George Washington visited campus and addressed students from the porch of Old North. The "College Diary," a daily handwritten account of campus events, recalls Washington's arrival alone on horseback to visit the campus where his grandnephews Bushrod and Augustine were students during his presidency. Including Washington, 14 US presidents have visited or spoken from the porch of Old North.

During the first decades of the 19th century, Georgetown's campus had "the air of a Southern plantation, with two rambling country schoolhouses" (Old South and Old North), according to Georgetown historian Joseph T. Durkin, SJ. In *The Catholics and Their Houses*, Leanda De Lisle and Peter Stranford indicate why this might have been so: "In keeping with the mood of English Catholicism in the early decades of the nineteenth century, the Jesuits avoided any confrontation by keeping a low profile [about their Catholic identity] and added small, solid if unspectacular buildings." John Carroll and his successors at Georgetown reflected this English sensitivity; it was not until the addition of Healy Hall in 1879 that any building at Georgetown featured an exterior cross. This 1831 painting, *Georgetown College from Trinity Steeple*, by James Alexander Simpson shows these "low profile" buildings.

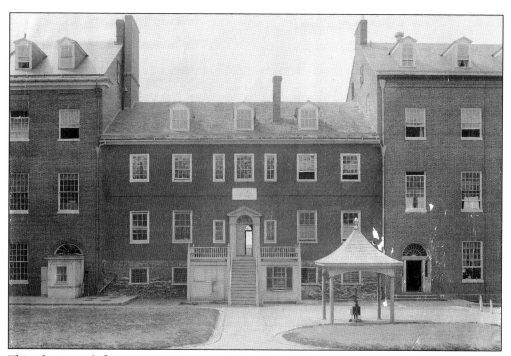

This photograph from 1874 shows Old South with the campus pump to the right of the main stairs. The Maguire building is on the left, and Isaac Hawkins Hall is to the right.

The south facade of Old North is shown in this 1874 photograph taken from the steps of Old South (previous image). Just to the left of the Old North entrance is a small structure, now gone, that first served as a porter's lodge, then a barbershop, and eventually a storage room.

Italian-born John Anthony Grassi, SJ (1812–1817), became president of Georgetown at a time when the school's financial circumstances and prospects for survival could not have been worse. John Carroll himself recommended in 1806 that the school be suspended for lack of funds. Emmett Curran writes that Carroll in 1812 confided to Charles Plowdon, SJ, that the college "has sunk to the lowest degree of discredit." The financial crisis at the college was constant. Influential Catholic elites sent their sons to Georgetown for education, but they did not provide financial support beyond tuition. Carroll's dream of an endowment funded by wealthy Catholics remained unfulfilled. Undeterred, Grassi set out to more than double enrollment, especially boarding students, to relieve the financial plight of the college. During Grassi's tenure, Georgetown received a federal charter and became, according to Curran, "the major domestic producer of clergy" for the church. In all, Grassi made significant progress to make Georgetown "the national college that Carroll had envisioned a generation earlier."

THIRTEENTH CONGRESS OF THE UNITED STATES;

AT THE THIRD SESSION,

Begun and held in the city of Washington, in the Territory of Columbia, on Monday the nineteenth day of September, one thousand eight hundred and fourteen.

AN ACT *Concerning the College of George Town in the District of Columbia.*

Be it enacted by the Senate and House of Representatives of the United States of America in Congress assembled, That *it shall and may be lawful for such persons, as now are, or from time to time may be, the president and Directors of the College of George Town, within the District of Columbia, to admit any of the Students belonging to said College or other persons meriting academical honors, to any degree in the faculties, arts, sciences, and liberal professions, to which persons are usually admitted in other colleges or universities of the United States; and to issue in an appropriate form, the diplomas or certificates, which may be requisite to testify the admission to such degrees.*

March 1. 1815
approved
James Madison

Langdon Cheves *Speaker of the House of Representatives.*

John Gaillard *President of the Senate pro tempore.*

I certify that this act, originated in the House of Representatives

Th. Dougherty Clerk

GENERAL SERVICES ADMINISTRATION
National Archives and Records Service

To all to whom these presents shall come, Greeting:

Georgetown's charter to grant academic degrees was approved by Pres. James Madison on March 1, 1815. Due to its location in the federal district, the "College of George Town in the District of Columbia" received a federal rather than a state charter to grant academic degrees, the first such federal charter granted to a school by Congress. Emmett Curran's review of John Carroll's correspondence revealed that Carroll did not seek a charter to grant academic degrees at first because he was concerned about government authorities interfering in the school's administration.

William Gaston, Georgetown's first student, arrived on campus in late 1791 at the age of 13. He left two years later due to illness and went on to graduate from the College of New Jersey (later Princeton University). While serving as a US congressman from North Carolina, Gaston presented the petition of the President and Directors of Georgetown College for a charter to grant academic degrees. Gaston Hall in Healy Hall is named in his honor.

The original Georgetown University seal was financed by a gift in 1798 from Justine Douat, a nurse who cared for students on campus. The 16 stars that surround the eagle date the seal's design to sometime between 1796 when Tennessee was admitted to the Union and 1802 when Ohio, the 17th state, was admitted. The Latin inscription surrounding the seal is *Collegium Georgiopolitanum Ad Ripas Potomaci in Marylandia*, indicating Georgetown's original location on the Potomac River in Maryland (the District of Columbia did not exist when Georgetown was founded). The Latin phrase *Utraque Unum* is taken from St. Paul's letter to the Ephesians and translates as "both one," signifying the unity of faith and knowledge. It is true that the Georgetown seal resembles the Great Seal of the United States, but there is no record indicating that permission was sought from the US government to use the eagle or other design elements for the Georgetown seal.

This painting by James Alexander Simpson depicts the campus in the 1830s after the addition of Gervase and Isaac Hawkins Hall. The campus itself had grown substantially in the first two decades of the 19th century when acreage surrounding the original campus came up for sale. Former Georgetown mayor John Threlkeld, from whom John Carroll purchased the first campus acre in 1789, was forced to sell his nearly 1,000-acre estate called Burleith to settle debts. An enterprising Pres. Francis Neale, SJ (1809–1812), purchased enough land from Threlkeld over two decades to extend the campus north to present-day Reservoir Road.

Thomas F. Mulledy, SJ, was twice president of Georgetown (1829–1837 and 1845–1848) and served as the first president of the College of the Holy Cross in Worcester, Massachusetts. As Georgetown president, Mulledy undertook a building campaign that added an infirmary (Gervase) and a large academic building (Isaac Hawkins Hall). Georgetown's need for new buildings was caused by a dramatic rise in enrollment, part of a strategy pursued by Mulledy to increase the prestige of the school. The new buildings were financed by debt. When Mulledy stepped down as Georgetown president to become the provincial of the Maryland Jesuits in 1838, he used his new authority to conduct the sale of 272 enslaved people owned by the Maryland Province. Mulledy then used part of the proceeds of the sale to pay down the college's debt, thereby violating a condition of sale set out by Jesuit superiors in Rome.

The 1838 sale did not end the presence of enslaved people in the Maryland Province or at Georgetown College. One enslaved person, Aaron Edmonson, was hired in 1859 as a domestic servant to work in the dormitories at Georgetown. The college accounts ledger records $12 per month paid for Edmonson's labor to Ann Green, his owner. Edmonson served at Georgetown until one month before he attained his freedom in 1862 at the age of 30.

This is the signature page of the "Articles of Agreement" dated June 1838 and signed by Thomas Mulledy, SJ, for the sale of 272 enslaved persons owned by the Jesuit province of Maryland to two plantation owners in Louisiana. The sale was controversial among Jesuits and initially opposed by Jesuit superiors in Rome, but permission to sell was granted by the society's superior general with conditions, three of which were: families were not to be separated, proceeds of the sale were not to be used to pay off debt or to pay operating expenses, and provisions were to be made for the religious practice of the enslaved people. Each condition was ultimately violated. What was described at the time as a tragic and disgraceful affair became the focus in 2015 of the Working Group on Slavery, Memory and Reconciliation, a group created by Pres. John J. DeGioia to inform the university's response to its legacy of slavery. (Archives of the Maryland Province of the Society of Jesus, on deposit at the Booth Family Center for Special Collections, Georgetown University.)

The Jesuit Cemetery on campus was originally located southeast of the Quad but was moved to its present site in 1854 to accommodate the construction of the Maguire building. The cemetery's first burial was in 1808, and all headstones are marked to indicate the decedent as coadjutor (Jesuit brother), sacerdos (Jesuit priest), or scholastic (Jesuit priest in training). Among those buried in the cemetery are 17 former university presidents.

This is the entrance to Anne Marie Becraft Hall, the oldest building on campus, built in 1792. Anne Marie Becraft was a free woman of color and Catholic nun who established a school in Georgetown in 1820 to educate girls of color. The small building was originally named for Pres. William McSherry, SJ (1838–1839), who was involved in the 1838 sale of enslaved persons owned by the Jesuit province of Maryland. The building was renamed in honor of Becraft in 2017 and houses the John Main Center for Meditation and Inter-religious Dialogue.

In 1834, one of Georgetown's first benefactors, Susan Decatur, made a gift of $7,000, money that her husband, Adm. Stephen Decatur, received from the Tripolitan War. The gift came with a provision that she receive an annuity of $630 per annum. She lived until 1860, however, so long that the annuities paid to her far exceeded her original gift.

The site of the White-Gravenor building was once occupied by the residence (right) of Susan Decatur and another structure called the Bachelors' house (left). Bachelors' house was so named because it served as a residence for secular teachers. In the foreground is part of today's Copley lawn, which was once the school's ball field and track.

27

This J.A. Simpson print appeared in the Washington, Goggin & Combs' "Catalogue of Officers and Students of Georgetown College for Year 1852-3." The Francis J. Heyden, SJ, Observatory, completed in 1844, was used in 1846 to determine the longitude of Washington, DC, the first such calculation for the nation's capital. The observatory was listed in the National Register of Historic Places in 1973.

James Curley, SJ, founded the Georgetown Observatory after securing funds for the project in 1841. The observatory, one of the first in the United States, was of Curley's own design, and he personally chose the location at the far western edge of the campus. Georgetown's astronomy department was the largest such program in the world by 1967. The astronomy major was phased out in 1972 due to lack of funding and, not incidentally, the observatory's proximity to the light pollution of Washington, DC.

Shown in this 1864 photograph is the oldest of Georgetown's student societies, the Sodality of the Immaculate Conception, founded in 1810. According to historian and alumnus Robert Easby-Smith, the Sodality was "placed under the patronage of the Blessed Virgin, having for its object the cultivation of virtue and piety." Easby-Smith continued, "It is composed of those of the more advanced Catholic students, who are distinguished among their comrades for their exemplary conduct." The Sodality of Georgetown held the first May Marian devotions celebrated in America.

1, Boyhood & youth; 2, y & early manh; 3 the Battle of Life in many lands; 4, (age 37 to 40), return & meet grown babies & toothless old drivelers who were the grandees of his boyhood. The mighty Unknown comes faded to maid & full of rasping, puritanical vinegar piety

The Adventures of Tom Sawyer.

Chap. I.

"Tom!"
No answer.
"Tom!"
No answer.
"Whats gone with that boy, I ~~wonder can that boy be,~~ I wonder? You Tom!"
No answer.
The old lady pulled her spectacles down & looked over them, about the room; then she put them up & looked under

Georgetown established archives in 1816, making it one of the oldest academic archives in the nation. Jesuit leaders directed that a fireproof facility be built to house important records and artifacts, eventually to include records of Georgetown College and the Maryland Province of Jesuits; timing suggests that the archives were created in response to the burning of the Capitol and White House in 1814. The archives today are part of the Booth Family Center for Special Collections. Among the objects housed in the Booth Center is Mark Twain's original manuscript for *The Aventures* [sic] *of Tom Sawyer* (pictured). The Booth Center also houses a first folio of Shakespeare, Gilbert Stuart's portrait of John Carroll, SJ, and a lock of George Washington's hair.

A dozen sacramental chalices from the earliest Catholic presence in the United States are among the most prized artifacts in the Booth Center. The Lancaster family chalice (pictured), from the Elizabethan era, could be disassembled and concealed in the saddlebag of an itinerant priest. The chalice, accompanied by its altar stone, was donated by Charles Calvert Lancaster and Malinda Jenkins Lancaster.

REV. JAMES RYDER, S. J.

James Ryder, SJ, served two terms as president of Georgetown, 1840–1845 and 1848–1851. Under Ryder, the college was incorporated by Congress in 1844, and the Medical School founded in 1851. Ryder was also a renowned Catholic preacher who publicly defended the practice of slavery. The Georgetown Slavery Archive records an August 1835 address in which Ryder describes abolitionists as "misguided abettors of disorder" who seek to upend "the peaceful, and contented, and secure condition of the Southern slave, under the gentle sway of an upright master."

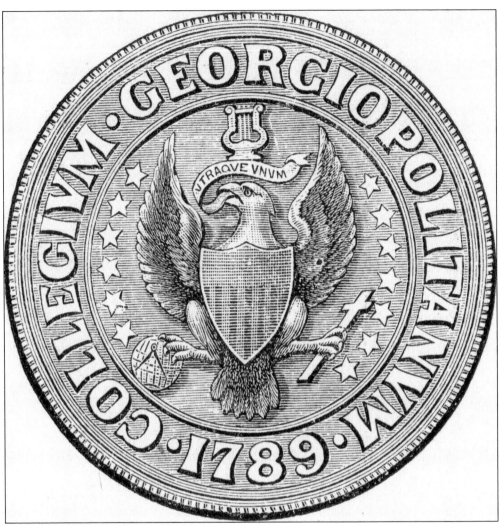

Georgetown was incorporated by Congress on June 10, 1844. Prior to this, the school operated without a corporate charter; the 1815 Act of Congress simply authorized Georgetown to grant academic degrees. This round version of the school seal was adopted sometime after incorporation and was used as the official seal until 1977. Although the seal's design closely resembles the 1798 version, it incorporates only 13 stars, an attempt to link Georgetown's founding more closely with that of the United States.

Two

THE "SECOND FOUNDING"

During a six-month tour of the United States in 1842, Charles Dickens visited the Georgetown campus. Dickens published his impressions from that day in *American Notes for General Circulation*. Although he found Washington, DC, (the place and the politicians) to be "disagreeable," his impressions of Georgetown's campus were quite favorable:

> At George Town, in the suburbs, there is a Jesuit College; delightfully situated, and, so far as I had an opportunity of seeing, well managed. Many persons who are not members of the Romish Church, avail themselves, I believe, of these institutions, and of the advantageous opportunities they afford for the education of their children. The heights of this neighbourhood, above the Potomac River, are very picturesque: and are free, I should conceive, from some of the insalubrities of Washington. The air, at that elevation, was quite cool and refreshing, when in the city it was burning hot.

Dickens's visit came at a time when Georgetown College, with 300 students, was one of the largest schools in the nation, according to Emmet Curran. Georgetown was also about to establish its first professional school, the Medical School, in 1851. The Law School, which followed in 1870, was promoted by Georgetown's medical faculty in concert with a post–Civil War movement to formalize the study of law in America. The medical faculty reasoned, as Curran wrote, that adding a law school "would have a favorable impact upon the reputation and prestige of the entire institution."

The Civil War prompted concerns that Georgetown would have to close when students, most of them from the South, left to enlist. The small number of remaining students lived and studied in Old North while Union troops occupied buildings on the south side of the Quad beginning in 1861. When the Civil War ended, Georgetown had survived what Curran described as "the most serious threat to its survival as an institution."

The presidency of Patrick F. Healy, SJ, Georgetown's "second founder," provided Georgetown with "a radically new sense of itself" after the Civil War, according to Curran. The new sense was portrayed visually by the monumental building that Healy commissioned. Equally significant, Healy brought Georgetown's professional schools of medicine and law into closer coordination with the college, in the style of other late-19th-century American universities.

This earliest-known photograph of the Georgetown campus dates to 1865. To the left stands Old North. To the right are Maguire, Old South, Isaac Hawkins Hall, and the Gervase Infirmary. Apart from the small cluster of buildings, the plantation-like campus provides no

hint of the expansive changes that would take place during the tenure of Patrick F. Healy, SJ, 10 years hence.

This photograph of the faculty of the medical department of Georgetown College was taken in the spring of 1868. The first classes of the medical department were held in May 1851, considered the founding date of the Medical School. Candidates for medical degrees at Georgetown were to be of good moral character, but a college education was not required. Students studied medicine for three or more years and attended at least one course that covered both practical anatomy and clinical instruction before graduating. Warwick Evans, the first graduate of the Medical School who became a professor of anatomy, is standing at far right. Standing at far left is Silas Loomis, a founder of Howard University College of Medicine.

Washington Oct 2nd 1849

To the President & Faculty of George Town College.

Gent:

The undersigned are about to establish a Medical College in the D. of Columbia, and respectfully ask, that, the right to confer the degree of M.D. granted to you by your charter, may be extended to them, they desire it to be understood as their object to constitute the Medical Department of George Town College, claiming the usual privilege of nominating the Professors of their Department

(Signed) N. Young, M.D.
F. Howard, M.D.
C. H. Lieberman, M.D.
Johnson Eliot M.D.

Frustrated by exclusionary practices of the medical department of Columbian College (now George Washington University) that controlled the city's only hospital, four local doctors submitted this petition to Pres. James Ryder, SJ, in fall of 1849 to establish a "medical department" that would be financially separate but grant degrees under the Georgetown College charter.

A few months after acquiring this warehouse at the corner of Twelfth and F Streets in 1849, the medical department acquired an adjacent lot to build a three-story building. By the time the first classes were offered two years later, the facility had grown to include an anatomical laboratory, a dispensary, two lecture rooms, and a six-bed infirmary.

QUARTERS OF THE SIXTY-NINTH (IRISH) REGIMENT NEW YORK STATE MILITIA, AT GEORGETOWN COLLEGE, D. C.—[SKETCHED BY OUR SPECIAL ARTIST.]

Artist Frank Leslie sketched this image of the campus being used as federal barracks for several regiments of the Union army during the Civil War. Pres. Abraham Lincoln visited the campus in May 1861 to review the 1,400 troops who made the Maguire building, Old South, and Isaac Hawkins Hall their temporary quarters. More than 1,000 Georgetown alumni served in the Civil War, 925 with the Confederate army and 216 with the Union army. By the end of the war, 106 Georgetown men had died. Although Georgetown's fortunes had brightened considerably in the years leading up to 1861, it was nearly ruined by the Civil War.

Three of the individuals convicted as accomplices in the 1865 conspiracy to assassinate President Lincoln were Georgetown alumni. Pictured at top left is David E. Herold, who attended Georgetown from 1855 to 1858. Known as the craftiest of Booth's accomplices, Herold escorted John Wilkes Booth after the assassination to the home of Dr. Samuel Mudd (top right, attended Georgetown 1861–1862), where Booth's broken leg was set. Samuel Arnold (right), who attended Georgetown in the mid-1840s, was implicated in a separate plot to kidnap Lincoln. Herold was hanged upon conviction. Mudd and Arnold were sentenced to life imprisonment but were pardoned in 1869 by Pres. Andrew Johnson.

Georgetown conferred only seven baccalaureate degrees in 1869, and this portrait of six of the graduates was commissioned for the occasion. It would be years before Georgetown returned to its pre–Civil War levels of 300-plus enrolled students. But Georgetown was nonetheless making important strides in its late-century quest to become a university, including the founding of its second professional school, the Law School, within the decade.

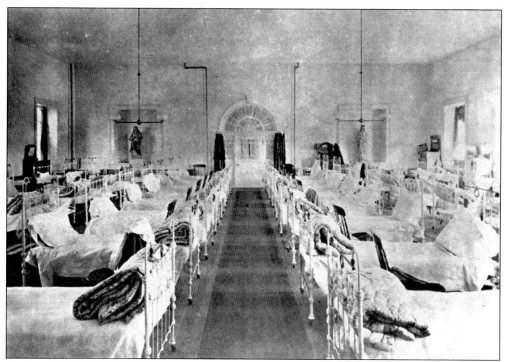

This image shows an open dormitory on the third floor of the Maguire building, completed in 1855 to house younger students enrolled in what was called the preparatory, or lower, school division of Georgetown College.

This photograph provides a detailed look at the campus as seen from the east in 1867. Readers will recognize the large stone wall bordering what is Thirty-Seventh Street today. The wall was extended to provide security for the campus after the Civil War when vagrancy, crime, and shanties, like those pictured in the foreground, sprung up nearby.

The first graduating class of the Georgetown Law School is pictured here on June 27, 1872. Creation of the Law School was approved in March 1870 in concert with a post–Civil War movement to formalize the study of law in America. The new professional school also furthered Georgetown's interest in becoming a university. The Law School's founding is directly traced to the efforts of Joseph M. Toner, a founder of the Medical School faculty. It was Toner who recruited three local lawyers to form the first Law School faculty.

The Law School held its first commencement on June 4, 1872, to confer 10 bachelor of law degrees at Lincoln Hall in Washington, DC. Like the Medical School, the Law School was financially independent from Georgetown College but conferred degrees under its academic charter. There were no prerequisites for admission, and until the 1930s, it was exclusively an evening program.

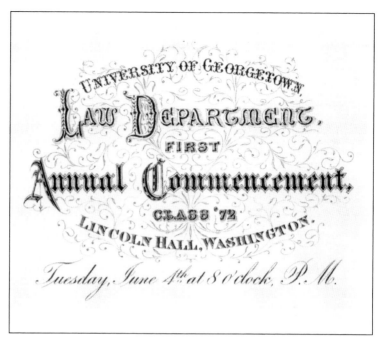

For the first two years of its existence, the Law School's classes were held in a building that was located on the present site of the National Gallery of Art East Building. Fourteen years after its founding in 1870, the Law School occupied an entire building for the first time, this former residence at Sixth and F Streets NW. The school would be housed here from 1884 until 1891.

A Maryland farmer named Joseph West became a Jesuit brother in 1818 and donated funds to purchase a sizable tract of land to expand the campus to the north and west. West himself developed the land, creating a beautiful series of paths, terraces, and trails that became known as "the Walks." The entrance to the Walks, pictured here in 1889, was near the present site of the White-Gravenor building.

These students were photographed in 1889 on one of the many bridges that crossed College Creek, a stream that ran through the Walks. Georgetown's campus was originally bisected by a deep and rocky ravine that ran from today's Reservoir Road to Canal Road. As the campus expanded westward, the stream was diverted, and landfill was used to create a mostly flat surface suitable for construction.

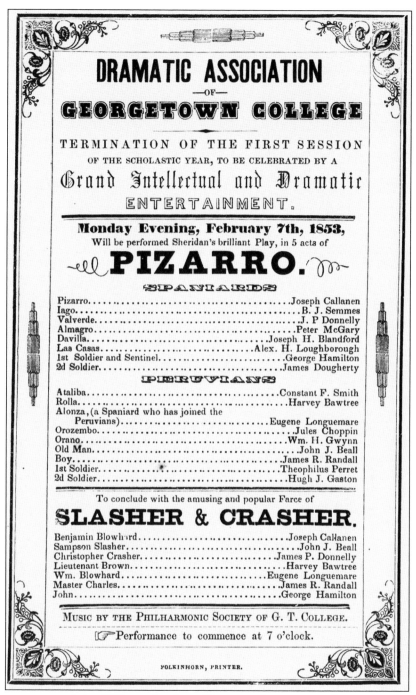

DRAMATIC ASSOCIATION
—OF—
GEORGETOWN COLLEGE

TERMINATION OF THE FIRST SESSION
OF THE SCHOLASTIC YEAR, TO BE CELEBRATED BY A

Grand Intellectual and Dramatic
ENTERTAINMENT.

Monday Evening, February 7th, 1853,
Will be performed Sheridan's brilliant Play, in 5 acts of

PIZARRO.
SPANIARDS

Pizarro	Joseph Callanen
Iago	B. J. Semmes
Valverde	J. P Donnelly
Almagro	Peter McGary
Davilla	Joseph H. Blandford
Las Casas	Alex. H. Loughborough
1st Soldier and Sentinel	George Hamilton
2d Soldier	James Dougherty

PERUVIANS

Ataliba	Constant F. Smith
Rolla	Harvey Bawtree
Alonza, (a Spaniard who has joined the Peruvians)	Eugene Longuemare
Orozembo	Jules Choppin
Orano	Wm. H. Gwynn
Old Man	John J. Beall
Boy	James R. Randall
1st Soldier	Theophilus Perret
2d Soldier	Hugh J. Gaston

To conclude with the amusing and popular Farce of

SLASHER & CRASHER.

Benjamin Blowhard	Joseph Callanen
Sampson Slasher	John J. Beall
Christopher Crasher	James P. Donnelly
Lieutenant Brown	Harvey Bawtree
Wm. Blowhard	Eugene Longuemare
Master Charles	James R. Randall
John	George Hamilton

MUSIC BY THE PHILHARMONIC SOCIETY OF G. T. COLLEGE.

☞ Performance to commence at 7 o'clock.

POLKINHORN, PRINTER.

This flyer announced the 1853 production of *Pizzaro*, featuring performer Hugh J. Gaston (C'55), the grandson of William Gaston. The Dramatic Association of Georgetown College, renamed the Mask and Bauble Dramatic Society in 1919, was then in its first season and is now the oldest continuously running college theater company in the nation. The name, Mask and Bauble, was chosen to indicate that the society would perform both tragedies and comedies.

Known as Georgetown's "second founder," Patrick F. Healy, SJ, served as president from 1873 to 1882. Healy was born in 1834 in Georgia to Michael Morris Healy, a wealthy white cotton planter, and Eliza Clark, an enslaved woman. As such, Patrick Healy was born a slave according to 19th-century Georgia law. So that his children could escape the consequences of enslavement, Michael Healy sent Patrick and his siblings to live and be educated in northern states and Europe. Healy came to Georgetown in 1866 as a Jesuit PhD to teach philosophy. The sudden death of Pres. John Early, SJ, in 1873 led to Healy's unexpected appointment as president, but once in office, Healy quickly introduced an audacious vision, one that would set Georgetown on a course to become a university, linking Georgetown College more closely with the recently established professional schools of medicine and law. As significantly, Healy transformed the physical character of the campus by constructing the massive Romanesque building that bears his name and serves as the visual symbol of the campus today.

This 1874 map of the city of Georgetown portrays a town that expanded rapidly during its first century. At far left is a reference to Georgetown College, bordered on the east by Warren Street, which was renamed Thirty-Seventh Street in 1895, along with most other streets in Georgetown, to conform with street naming conventions of Washington, DC. This was the Georgetown College campus that Patrick Healy would transform.

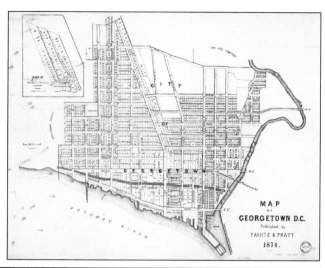

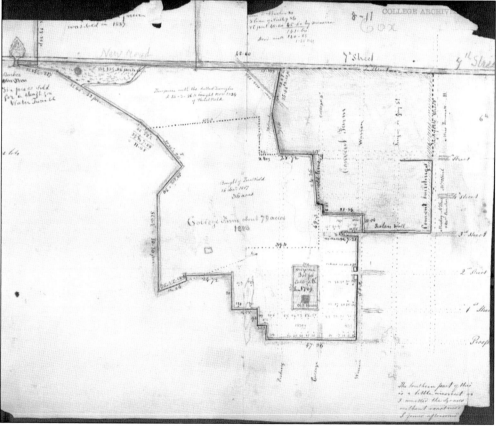

This rarely seen hand-drawn map from 1888 details the incremental growth of campus through land purchased from John Threlkeld, who owned the farmland surrounding the original campus. At bottom center is a mark for the site of Georgetown's first building, Old South. To the right is the Visitation convent and school, founded in 1799. At top, the map indicates that Georgetown owned 76 acres north of Reservoir Road. That tract, known as Hickorynut Hill, was sold in 1887 to pay down debt incurred when Healy Hall was built.

This is a preliminary study for Healy Hall, submitted in 1876 by the architectural firm of Smithmeyer and Peltz, the same firm that designed the Thomas Jefferson building of the Library of Congress. Although similar in many ways to Healy Hall's final design, this original plan featured a twin spire at the center and anticipated the demolition of Old North to make room for a wing that would extend westward from the new building. The cost of executing this extensive plan eliminated it from final consideration.

Smithmeyer and Peltz submitted this final design for Healy Hall in 1877. The proposal depicts the ornate Romanesque style that would become the building's signature feature. Perhaps equal in importance to the building's architecture was its orientation. As Emmett Curran notes, "For the first time in its history the university was constructing a building that fronted not the river but the city, as if to state visually its intention of becoming an enduring Catholic university in the capital of the United States." The landmark structure added 110,000 square feet of classroom and dormitory space—more than all of the buildings on campus combined—and visibly symbolized Patrick Healy's aspirations for Georgetown.

This photograph was taken in 1879, when exterior construction of Healy Hall was nearing completion. The interior of the "New Building," as it was called, (it was later named Healy Hall against the wishes of Patrick Healy) would remain incomplete for 20 years. The costs of constructing Healy Hall far exceeded original estimates. As Joseph Durkin, SJ, wrote, "The Healy Building's completion was a financial near-miracle. It was begun with an insufficient loan, halted periodically by empty coffers, once almost totally canceled and finally achieved by tapping the food and clothing budget of the resident Jesuits." Indeed, the costs of the building were four times the amount approved by Jesuit superiors in Rome. To conserve money without compromising the building's grand design, Healy left large parts of it temporarily unfinished, including Gaston Hall, Riggs Library, and the two east entrance porticoes.

Starting in 1901, Brother Francis Schroen, SJ, decorated most of the public spaces of Healy Hall, including the entranceway, parlors, and most significantly, the interior of Gaston Hall. Pictured at left is the landing of Healy's grand staircase. Here, Schroen painted images that link learning (*scientia*) and religion (*religio*) with the "light of the world," (*lux mundi*), inscribed on a blazing torch above the emblem of the Society of Jesus (IHS). Prominent in Schroen's decorative ceiling scrolls are leaves from beech, oak, sycamore, and chestnut trees that were common on the college grounds.

As directed by Patrick Healy, the third and fourth floors of Healy Hall were designed to house older students in single rooms. This 1901 photograph shows how one student decorated his Healy dormitory room.

The Chemical Lecture Room in Healy Hall was photographed in 1894. From about 1838, students were taught chemistry and other subjects in natural philosophy at Georgetown, but the school did not offer a bachelor of science degree until 1879. Indeed, Georgetown's curriculum was decidedly classical. The same set of courses united structurally by Latin and Greek were required of all students. Elective studies, as they are known today, did not exist.

Located within Healy Hall, the Coleman Museum is seen here in 1889. The museum was filled with eclectic natural history specimens, including a stuffed bald eagle that was moved to the stage in Gaston Hall for commencement and other important proceedings. Later, in 1931, the museum was closed, most of the contents were given away, and the space was remodeled into a four-room suite for the president's office.

The Philodemic Room serves as home to Georgetown's Philodemic Society for debate and literature, the school's oldest non-religious student group and the only student group granted its own room in Healy Hall. The Philodemic Society was organized in 1830 with the aim of cultivating eloquence devoted to liberty.

Georgetown College,
May 3rd 1880.

My dear Sir,

I enclose a copy of the projected constitution of the Alumni Society of Georgetown College, based mainly upon the one that now obtains in the University of Virginia.

In a short time a preliminary meeting of some of the alumni will be called for its ratification subject to such amendments as may be deemed advisable.

To this end I invite you to make a careful perusal of the enclosed document. You will be informed of the time and place of the meeting.

Yours truly,
P. F. Healy S.J.

This May 1880 letter from Patrick Healy to alumni prompted the first annual meeting of the "Society of Alumni" on June 23, 1881, and the founding of the modern Georgetown University Alumni Association. At the meeting, a committee was appointed to raise funds to complete the "Aula Maxima" (later Gaston Hall). Alumnus R.T. Merrick affirmed Healy's request for alumni support: "The college which nurtured us in youth should now in its need receive some reciprocation in the way of aid from the gathered strength of our manhood. This cooperation then will bring this venerated institution into successful competition with the most favored Universities in our English-speaking people." The first president of the Society of Alumni was William Corcoran, co-founder of the Corcoran and Riggs bank, who attended Georgetown in 1813.

With construction funds exhausted, the auditorium space that would become Gaston Hall remained unfinished for 20 years. An 1879 *Washington Post* article described the "harshness of the incompletion," with "rough, un-plastered walls . . . and great hewn beams stretching out nakedly from the sides." It was a barn-like space. The Gaston interior improved in stages as funds became available.

In the early 1880s, Gaston Hall was furnished with chairs and a temporary stage so it could be used for commencement and other public events.

Georgetown alumni raised the funds necessary to finish the interior carpentry of Gaston Hall. In 1896, the room was described in the *College Journal* as "paneled in white Florida pine, with massive polished girders, and an elaborate metal cornice of beautiful design in Gothic arches and brackets finished in bronze." During this phase of completion, bunting and plants were brought in to enhance the stage and hide the unpainted plaster walls.

This photograph was taken shortly after the murals decorating Gaston Hall were completed in 1901 by Brother Schroen. Most prominent in the room are the large allegorical paintings flanking the arched windows behind the stage. Prominently located below the paintings in the center of the stage wall is the Latin phrase *Ad maiorem Dei gloriam inque hominum salutem* (For the greater glory of God and the salvation of humanity). *Ad majorem Dei gloriam* (AMDG) is the motto of the Society of Jesus. Other painted features of the room include crests from 60 Jesuit institutions throughout the world. Above the crests is the word "Wisdom," and seldom noticed on the eastern wall at the back of the hall is, in twin fashion, the word "Virtue," linking "Wisdom" with a moral life.

Prof. John Glavin (C'64), an expert in Georgetown architecture and history, has studied the meanings of the murals that flank the Gaston stage. Of the first mural, Glavin writes, "Faith is flanked by Morality, holding the ten commandments, and Patriotism, specifically American Patriotism as can be seen from the American flag as cape and the image on the shield. Crucially, her sword is aimed not against but in front of Faith, as guard and protector. This image seems addressed to the remains of anti-Catholicism in America, arguing that the American Republic and Catholic Georgetown are not enemies but collaborators in a larger vision of the meaningful life."

About the second mural, Glavin writes, "Alma Mater, clearly Georgetown in Blue and Gray, offers exactly equal laurels to both Art and Science, virtual mirror images of each other. If the first allegory [Faith, Morality and Patriotism] centers on America, the second treats the Church in its relation to contemporary knowledge. Georgetown is not afraid of, indeed honors, the new sciences, which throughout the nineteenth century had troubled so many orthodox churchmen. Both Art and Science are fit partners in the Jesuit curriculum."

Riggs Library in Healy Hall is one of only a few cast-iron libraries existing in the nation. Cast iron was attractive as a building material for library interiors at the time because it was fireproof. The Historic American Buildings Survey, housed in the Library of Congress, details the library's rich interior, particularly the four-story cast-iron book stacks decorated with crosses and decorative squares of Gothic foliage. The library was funded by a gift in 1889 from E. Francis Riggs, whose father was a founder of Corcoran & Riggs bank. The ornate space served as Georgetown's main library until Lauinger Library opened in 1970.

E. Francis Riggs named the library as a memorial to his late father and to his late brother, a Georgetown graduate. Located between the entrance doors is a plaque in Latin that in translation reads, "When Elisha Francis Riggs had finished this library at his own expense, he chose it to bear the name of his father, George W[ashington], and of his brother, Thomas L[awrason], and to serve as a perpetual token that he holds them in affectionate remembrance. The president and directors of Georgetown College, in grateful accord with this loving thought, have erected this tablet in the year of our Lord eighteen hundred and ninety-one." The ornate oak library furniture seen here was donated by Francis Riggs.

This photograph was taken in 1891 before books were moved into the library. Visible at the ceiling line are shields that remain today, displaying the seals of the Riggs family, the United States, the Society of Jesus, and Georgetown University.

The cornerstone for Dahlgren Chapel of the Sacred Heart was laid on May 19, 1892. The cross-shaped, English Gothic–style building was made of red brick and Indiana stone. The chapel was the gift of alumnus John Vinton Dahlgren (C'89) and his wife, Elizabeth Drexel Dahlgren, in memory of their first-born son, Joseph, who died as an infant. Dahlgren Chapel was the first building on campus funded entirely from external gifts and the first named for a non-Jesuit. Elizabeth was the granddaughter of renowned Philadelphia banker Franz Martin Drexel and the cousin of St. Katharine Drexel.

The interior of Dahlgren Chapel is finished in Georgia pine, which can be seen in the forms of the hammer beams overhead. All of the chapel's stained-glass windows were made in Munich, Germany, under the personal direction of Elizabeth Dahlgren.

The visual center of the chapel's main window is the Sacred Heart, patron of the chapel. On the left of the Sacred Heart, facing the altar, is the Virgin Mary, and on the right is St. Joseph. At far right is St. John the Evangelist (patron saint of John Dahlgren) and at far left is St. Elizabeth of Hungary (patron saint of Elizabeth Dahlgren). The uppermost center rose is the emblem of the Society of Jesus (IHS). The right roundel portrays St. Margaret Mary Alocoque, whose apparitions inspired devotion to the Sacred Heart. The left roundel depicts St. Claude de la Colombiere, SJ, St. Margaret Mary Alocoque's confessor. (Photograph by Phil Humnicky.)

The Society of Alumni gathered on February 21, 1889, to celebrate Georgetown's centennial on the still-unfinished north portico of Healy Hall. To the right of the entrance hangs a banner listing Calverton 1640, Newtown 1677, Bohemia 1740, and Georgetown 1789, all names and dates associated with Jesuit schools in early Maryland. To the left hangs a banner with verses of Russian poetry in honor of Russia's harboring the Society of Jesus during its suppression.

As president from 1888–1898, J. Havens Richards, SJ, was instrumental in advancing Patrick Healy's ambition to establish Georgetown as a university. Emmett Curran describes Richards as an "imaginative and far-sighted leader" who wanted faculty to be experts in their field, especially in emerging disciplines that characterized late-19th-century American universities. Richards is credited with a number of achievements. He pushed for more rigorous admissions standards and a full-time dean at the Law School, instituted a day program at the Medical School, and encouraged the establishment of Georgetown's first hospital. Richards also launched what Curran describes as the first "systematic effort" to raise money from alumni, starting with an appeal at the centennial celebration in 1889. Richards's fundraising efforts fell short, but he made clear to alumni that Georgetown would never realize its full potential as a university without a permanent endowment that reflected "the growing wealth among the Catholic elite [Georgetown alumni in particular]" and their "more active interest in higher educational work."

Robert Collier graduated from Georgetown with a bachelor of arts degree in 1894. While at Georgetown, he was the editor-in-chief of the student periodical, the *College Journal*, and wrote the words to Georgetown's official college song, "Sons of Georgetown, Alma Mater."

Condé Nast, an 1894 graduate of Georgetown, first worked as a business manager at *Collier's Weekly* (thanks to his college roommate Robert Collier). Nast went on to found the publishing empire that bears his name. While a student, Nast was captain of the tennis team, manager of the early basketball team, and in 1891, the first president of the student government of the college.

Before organized athletic teams emerged on campus, handball, tennis, and track were popular recreational activities for students. Erected in 1897, the junior students' handball alley pictured here stood on the site of today's Village A.

Students gathered in front of the college wall for Field Day in October 1891. The intramural sporting event was held each year in the late 1800s before intercollegiate sports teams took root on campus.

The student government at Georgetown has its roots in the Georgetown University Athletic Association, which adopted a constitution in 1874 calling for the election of officers to lead athletic activities. By 1880, the meetings of the Athletic Association functioned as an informal student government called the Yard. (The Yard was another way of referring to the Quad where the students gathered.) The Yard president was elected by students and was referred to in *The Hoya* in 1920 as "the official head of the student body." In this 1901 photograph, junior members of the Yard assemble casually on the steps of Healy Hall.

Baseball is Georgetown's oldest organized sport and began in 1869 with two baseball clubs called the Stonewalls and Quicksteppers. The school's first intercollegiate baseball game was played on May 10, 1870, against Columbian College (now George Washington University). The 1899 intercollegiate baseball championship title was bestowed on Georgetown by the *Boston Herald*.

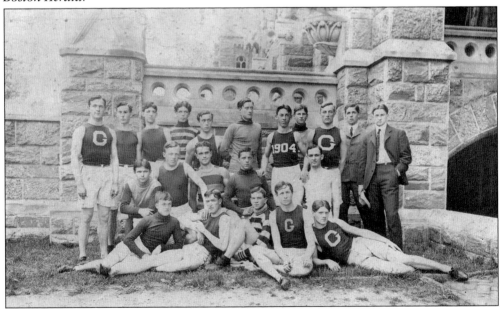

Track and field was among the earliest organized sports at Georgetown (1893), along with football, baseball, and crew. Over the years, track stood out for its competitive success. The Hoyas had an intercollegiate outdoor track champion in every running and field event except the pole vault from 1896 through 1952.

The Georgetown rowing team was photographed at Poughkeepsie, New York, 14 years after the founding of the Georgetown Boat Club in 1876 by students John Agar, T.P. Kernan, and James Dolan. In a sport that required bright colors to distinguish boats from the shoreline, intercollegiate crews adopted colors to identify their jerseys and racing shells. Georgetown's rowing team commissioned a group of Georgetown Visitation students to make blue and gray banners for their racing shells during competition; the colors, symbolizing the reuniting of the North and South after the Civil War, were soon widely accepted as Georgetown's official school colors.

In this 1886 photograph, the rowing team is on the Potomac River in front of the campus. The Georgetown Boat Club (as the rowing team was then called) relied heavily on support from the Potomac Boat Club, founded in 1869 for recreational rowers. The president of the Potomac Boat Club, Claude Zappone, was the rowing team's first coach and considered to be the father of the team. Students raced in shells gifted to them from the Potomac Boat Club.

Georgetown's first football game against an outside team was played on Old Varsity Field in 1887 against the Emerson Institute, a Washington, DC, prep school founded in 1852 to prepare local boys for attendance at Harvard. Georgetown prevailed, 46-6.

Taken in 1889, this is the earliest known photograph of a Georgetown football team. Football was a popular but controversial college sport. With little protective equipment and few safety rules, players were frequently injured, sometimes fatally. Football was canceled at Georgetown following the 1894 death of George "Shorty" Bahen from injuries sustained on the field. Football resumed in 1897 but was suspended several times again, not only because it was dangerous, but also because the costs of fielding a team were considered prohibitive.

Athletic teams at Georgetown have had canine mascots since the early 20th century. The dogs of Georgetown have included Boston bull terriers named Jazz Bo and Stubby, a great Dane named Butch, and bulldogs, all named Jack. The Hoya nickname was first attributed to Jazz Bo, a mascot in the 1920s and to date the only female canine to serve in that role. Student cheers of "Go Hoya!" for Jazz Bo's halftime show pushing a football across the field with her nose influenced a headline writer from *The Hoya* in 1928 to be the first to refer to Georgetown's football team as the Hoyas rather than the Hilltoppers, as they were known at the time. An early canine mascot is pictured in this 1911 pregame face-off with the University of Virginia. (University of Virginia Archives.)

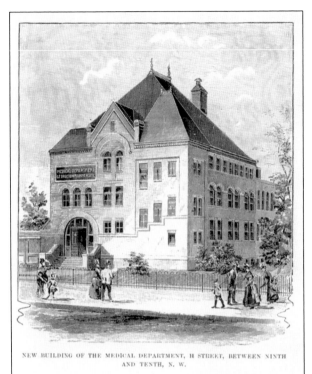

NEW BUILDING OF THE MEDICAL DEPARTMENT, H STREET, BETWEEN NINTH AND TENTH, N. W.

The Medical School building at 920 H Street, pictured here in 1889, was the first building owned by the Medical School. The school was previously housed at F and Twelfth Streets NW and later at Tenth and E Streets. These downtown locations proved problematic at times. As the *Washington Post* reported in 1888, complaints from neighbors about "objectionable smells" from the dissecting room led to demands that the Medical School move from the city center. The school remained downtown, however, until 1930, when it relocated to Georgetown's Main Campus, closer to Georgetown Hospital.

This building at 506 E Street was the first building owned by the Law School but the fifth that it occupied after its founding in 1870. Opened in November 1891, the building was described by the *College Journal* as "a marvel of beauty, elegance, and convenience." With the new facility, Law School enrollment jumped from 145 in 1886 to 280 students in 1891, making Georgetown the third-largest law school in the nation. It was expanded numerous times and remained the Law School's home until 1971.

Three

THE NEW CENTURY

Intercollegiate rivalries around the start of the 20th century, especially in football, prompted fans to invent distinctive fight songs and cheers. "Hoya, Hoya, Saxa!" emerged by 1894 as the Georgetown cheer. Tradition holds that "Hoya, Saxa!" is a combination of the Latin *hoia* and the Greek *saxa*, which together are translated to mean "What Rocks!" The origin of the cheer is uncertain, but it may refer to an early intramural baseball team called the Stonewalls, a large stone wall fronting the campus, or the fact that Georgetown's football team was said to have a "stone wall" defense. Students may have associated "Hoya, Saxa!" with the baseball team, the campus wall, the football team, or all three. Regardless, the cheer took root, newspaper reporters started referring to Georgetown's sports teams as the Hoyas in 1928, and the tradition carried on.

Beyond college cheers, Georgetown's development as a university stalled at the turn of the 20th century. According to Emmett Curran, the cause was "a lack of both stability and strong leadership in the period." Patrick Healy's immediate successors implemented changes to ensure that Georgetown would be a university, not just, as Curran observed, "an overgrown college or collection of colleges." But any systematic planning or vision of the institution as a university departed with Pres. Havens Richards in 1898. The lack of progress in the college would last two decades.

Growth and progress did not stall at the Medical School or the Law School, however. The Medical School created two new programs, a dental department (1901) and the Training School for Nurses (1903). The Law School expanded to become among the largest in the nation; it hired full-time faculty and established admissions standards that were consistent with the nation's leading law schools. The upshot of these thriving professional schools was to strengthen Georgetown as a university by their success, even if the College was struggling to advance.

This photograph, taken in 1888 from the south tower of Healy Hall, shows, to the right, the Potomac River docks used to transfer coal from canal barges to riverboats. Visible in the foreground is the hilly terrain on which early houses near the campus were built. In the 1870s, a large public works project was undertaken to remove hills and level ravines in the area. This resulted in flatter streets in front of the campus but forced homeowners to install steps that led up or down from the new street elevation, a characteristic that remains today.

Healy Hall is shown with several cows grazing nearby on what is today Copley Lawn. The exact date of the photograph is unknown; however, the presence of the central and north porches of Healy (completed by 1889) and the absence of Ryan Gymnasium (completed in 1906) suggest a turn-of-the-century date.

Ryan Hall was dedicated in 1904, replacing Georgetown's first structure, Old South. The new building was funded by Ida M. Ryan, wife of Thomas Ryan and the mother of two Georgetown students at the time. Ryan Hall faced the Potomac River and was designed with four two-story Ionic columns of Indiana limestone, intended to make the building stand out when viewed from the river; its three verandas provided spectacular panoramic views. The building was filled with modern conveniences like electric lights, open-work plumbing, and a hot-water heating system.

These two cooks, photographed at their job around 1906, were part of the campus staff serving students.

The kitchen in Ryan Hall filled the entire basement. It was divided into sections that included the cooking area, bakeshop, cold storage, dessert room, and workmen's dining room.

The interior walls of the Ryan Hall refectory were painted in 1916 by Francis Schroen, the Gaston Hall artist. Schroen decorated the walls with the names of notable Georgetown alumni as well as the names of former students who died in the Mexican-American and Civil Wars. Adding to the refinement of the refectory, according to a 1905 newspaper clipping in the Georgetown Archives, Ida Ryan donated delftware and paid for waiters to serve meals as a way to "cultivate a love of the beautiful" among students.

The Medical School faculty advised that integrating an operating hospital into the curriculum would greatly enhance the school's standing, and in early 1897, plans were drawn up to build Georgetown's first hospital on land donated by banker E. Francis Riggs at Thirty-Fifth and N Streets. The hospital was converted to a student dormitory in the 1980s, but the ambulance bay, visible at lower right, is still a feature of the building today.

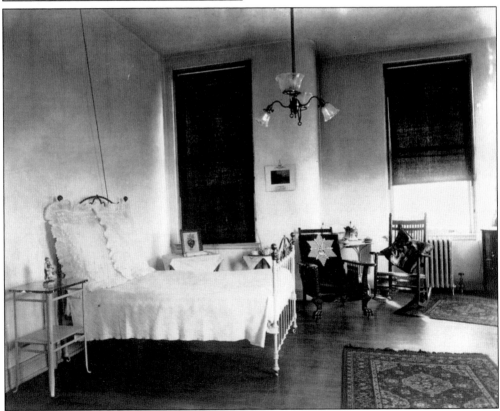

This patient room at Georgetown Hospital was photographed in 1906. The hospital received patients regardless of race, creed, or color, but patient rooms were segregated. The original hospital was expanded to encompass most of the city block that would be called East Campus.

Pictured in 1906 are the first graduates of the Georgetown Training School for Nurses. Founded in 1903 and originally run by the Sisters of Saint Francis, the School of Nursing and Health Studies, as it was later named, trained nurses for the growing Georgetown Hospital.

This photograph shows the operating room at Georgetown Hospital in 1906. The *College Journal* at the time described the white-tiled operating room and the glass operating tables as the "latest design and equipped with all the modern improvements."

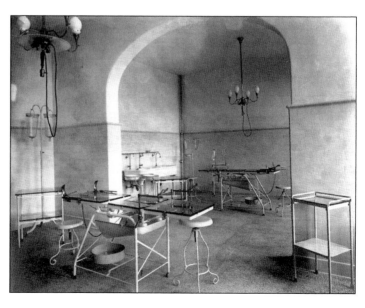

This turn-of-the-century photograph shows Ryan Gymnasium under construction. Somewhat incidental to the subject of this photograph are the wide-open windows of Old North and Healy Hall—both probably stifling hot in summertime Washington, DC. The summer heat was surely a factor in activities at Georgetown before air conditioning. In fact, minutes from the 1894 Annual Meeting of Alumni made note of the "flies and heat" that plagued their June meeting.

This photograph offers an unusual perspective of the Old North building. The original foundation lines, seen here from the west, became visible when the Quad was lowered in 1892 for the construction of Dahlgren Chapel. By 1926, this side of the building would be obscured by the New North building.

Soon after construction of Healy Hall was completed, a special area was set aside in front of the building for a statue honoring John Carroll. Alumni raised funds to commission a bronze statue, which was unveiled on May 4, 1912.

This photograph was taken soon after alumnus Edward Douglas White, chief justice of the Supreme Court, conducted the dedication ceremony for the new Carroll statue. The statue unveiled at the May 4 event, however, was a fake. Days before the ceremony, the foundry reported that the statue would not be ready in time. Rather than cancel the event, university leaders had a plaster copy of the statue made and painted it brown. The plaster replica remained in place for several weeks until the bronze statue was installed, under cover of darkness to escape notice.

Ryan Gymnasium opened in 1906, made possible through a gift from Ida M. Ryan, who had earlier funded the building of Ryan Hall. The gymnasium was designed as a facility for multiple sports and fitness. The basketball team played home games in Ryan for a time, but there was little room for spectators, and the elevated track around the perimeter made corner shots impossible. The elevated track was removed in 1939, but it was not until the opening of McDonough Arena in 1951 that basketball games returned to campus. Ryan Gymnasium is today a part of the Davis Performing Arts Center.

Georgetown's first intercollegiate basketball team was formed in 1907, with five of the seven players coming from the Law School. The early years of the team were remarkably successful, with only one losing season among the first 19.

This photograph shows the Quad as it appeared at the turn of the 20th century. At lower right is a replica of the original campus water pump, installed to memorialize the daily experience of the earliest students, who at dawn each day used water from the pump to wash their face and hands before daily mass and classes.

Four

THE WORLD WARS
AND GLOBAL FOCUS

Two world wars, an economic depression, and America's emergence as a global power were defining events for the nation and for Georgetown in the 20th century. Pres. John B. Creeden, SJ, positioned Georgetown at the close of World War I to respond to the global economic and political forces that were reshaping the world. Creeden's choice as the first dean and regent of the School of Foreign Service, Edmund A. Walsh, SJ, developed a school that elevated foreign service to a vocation worthy of study and trained students to work in the foreign service and international commerce five years before the Rogers Act created the Foreign Service of the United States.

The Greater Georgetown building campaign of Pres. W. Coleman Nevils, SJ, provided facilities that were needed to support the growth of programs for the six schools that made up Georgetown University after 1919. Nevils transformed the campus in ways that first affected the Medical School by locating the new Medical-Dental Building at the far northwestern corner of campus, contrary to earlier plans to build the Medical-Dental Building on East Campus adjacent to the original Georgetown Hospital. Greater Georgetown also moved athletic fields away from the main entrance of the campus to make way for an academic quadrangle that included Copley Hall and the White-Gravenor building. The effects of the Great Depression stalled Nevils's further plans to relocate the Law School to campus from downtown.

Five years before the Rogers Act created the Foreign Service of the United States, Georgetown founded the School of Foreign Service (SFS) in 1919 "to promote peace through understanding," as stated in founding documents and speeches. Edmund A. Walsh, SJ (pictured), was the first dean and regent of the SFS and is commonly considered to be its "founder." Walsh, however, credited Pres. John B. Creeden, SJ (1918–1924), as the person who conceived of the school, along with Constantine McGuire, an assistant secretary in the treasury department. The SFS, named for Walsh in 1958, responded to a postwar need for students trained to work in the foreign service and international commerce. Both the Institute of Languages and Linguistics (1949) and the McDonough School of Business (1957) were originally part of the SFS.

Pictured is the opening lecture of the SFS led by Edmund Walsh in February 1919. The initial program of 70 students and 17 faculty grew within the year to 300 students and 33 faculty. The SFS was an evening-only program until 1926. Some graduates of the first class entered diplomatic service, but more than half went to work for global businesses.

Final oral examinations for the SFS were held in the Constitution Room in Healy Hall, a room designed by Edmund Walsh. The murals in the room depict the signing of the Declaration of Independence in 1776 and *The Settlement of Maryland by Lord Baltimore*. The figure imparting the benediction in the latter mural is Andrew White, SJ.

This 1918 photograph shows uniformed Georgetown Student Army Training Corps (SATC) students assembled in Ryan Gymnasium. Following the US entry into World War I, Pres. Woodrow Wilson authorized the creation of the SATC. Hundreds of Georgetown students entered the corps and, at the age of 21, were inducted as officers of the Army or Navy.

This photograph from 1918, taken by a US Army airplane, is the first aerial view of campus. When the photograph ran in the May 1920 issue of the *London News*, the headline declared Georgetown to be "the Versailles of America." At the time, the campus was almost exclusively centered around the Quad. New North was not yet built, but the roof of Ryan Gymnasium is visible, as are the ball field and grandstands. Practice fields occupy the present site of Village A and Lauinger Library.

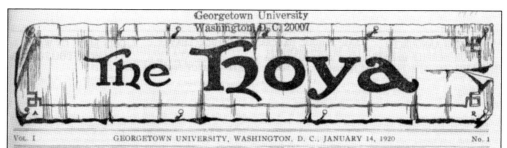

Georgetown University
Washington, D. C. 20007

VOL. I   GEORGETOWN UNIVERSITY, WASHINGTON, D. C., JANUARY 14, 1920   No. 1

OFFICERS NAMED FOR SECOND HALF

Major Hobson Makes Changes In Georgetown Unit, R. O. T. C.

New officers for the Unit have been announced through a special order issued by Major Hobson. The previous appointments and assignments of cadet officers and non-commissioned officers have been revoked. The new organization is to go into effect at once.

When the companies are assembled as a unit, that is, to drill and execute the various duties prescribed for the battalion, the following assigned officers will take their respective posts:

COMPANY A.

Captain Paul Etzel.
First Lieutenant J. A. Butler.
Second Lieutenant H. L. McElhinny.
First Sergeant J. G. Starr.
Supply Sergeant H. C. Verkamp.
J. S. McNulty.

Sergeants:
G. E. Helfrich.
J. S. Donahue.
C. J. O'Neill.

Corporals:
J. D. Curtin.
E. Pringle.
H. D. Moran.
J. B. Roddy.
D. J. McSorley.
F. P. Walsh.

COMPANY B.

Captain E. T. Butler.
First Lieutenant G. M. Carney.
Second Lieutenant C. A. Williams.
First Sergeant Paul Page.
Supply Sergeant T. J. Tyne.

Sergeants:
W. D. McNamara.
J. O'D. Hanlon.
J. R. Finn.
J. F. Little.

Corporals:
F. E. Kundtz.
C. C. Walsh.
A. Sheridan.
F. D. O'Connor.
W. A. Englehorn.
J. A. McGowan.

On days when the companies are assembled according to classes with regard to the first and second year of the basic course, the following officers and non-commissioned officers will be in charge:

COMPANY A.

Captain M. E. Maloney.
First Lieutenant N. A. McKenna.
Second Lieutenant H. B. Brennan.
First Sergeant A. D. Malley.
Supply Sergeant E. J. Schneider.

Sergeants:
W. T. Cusiff.
C. S. Shuperns.
J. H. Donahue.
S. J. Pauley.

Corporals:
C. Lowndes.
K. Lynch.
R. C. McCane.
D. E. McGuire.

COMPANY B.

Captain R. V. Tonsatt.
First Lieutenant H. M. McElhinny.
Second Lieutenant C. A. Williams.
First Sergeant J. R. McDonough.

LOOK WHO'S HERE!

We knew that Georgetown was big enough for THE HOYA.
So we have made THE HOYA big enough for Georgetown.
THE HOYA is going to prove a howling success.
Hence there is a crying need for material.
All NEWS is always material—the very best sort.
And a good story—like a good man—is hard to find.
Humorous verse will be received with open boat-hooks.
All drawings and cartoons will have the run of the shop.
Every Georgetown man is a member of the staff.
We want news first—this is a newspaper.
Then we want original wise cracks in words or pictures.
Send us the funniest thing you know of.
How about a picture of your room-mate?
Some college papers are like Swiss babies.
They depend on one or two goats for support.
This paper is going to be a community baby.
Everybody takes a try at it.
Otherwise we had better go get the little white hearse.
The Kewpie will only play a one-night stand, unless he gets a lot of nourishment.
Let's all make a noise like real food.
That will drown out the slow music.

FATHER BECKER'S FUNERAL HELD

Incidents In Life of Beloved Treasurer Recalled by Hoya Writer.

The funeral of Rev. James B. Becker, S. J., the beloved treasurer of the University for 18 years, was held from Dahlgren Chapel at 9 o'clock Saturday morning, December 20, during the Christmas holidays. Representatives from the clergy of Washington, many prominent business men, and the relatives and numerous friends of Father Becker were present. Rev. John B. Creeden, S. J., President of the University, was the celebrant of the mass. Burial was in the cemetery on the college grounds.

The next issue of the Journal, the University magazine, gives a detailed account of the life of Father Becker, who was one of the oldest of the faculty. In passing, however, it is the great privilege of THE HOYA to attempt in a humble way to voice the esteem in which the venerable treasurer was held by the men of the college.

Father Becker was one of that rare type that gets close to the hearts of men, one who is not only highly respected and admired from a distance, but known intimately and loved with a degree of open-hearted friendship that only the very greatest of earth can demand.

Everybody knew Father Becker. Everybody loved him. The news of his death came while the juniors were having their specimens in minor logic. The seniors, as is the custom, were also present. The pall of gloom, the grief and sorrow that settled over the two upper classes that morning gave mute testimony of the greatness of the man. Everywhere throughout the dormitories, in the graduate schools, the news traveled, "Father Becker is dead," and in the college store even her pans and pots as she made the egg sandwiches and added an extra lump of sugar to the coffee, old Alice, the colored "Mammy," wiped the tears away as they streamed down her generous cheeks, sobbing as though her heart would break for the man who was everybody's friend.

Not only the accomplishments of great deeds, nor the hours of business sagacity, and the like display the greatness of a man. Sometimes the greatness of his successes do not reveal the heart underneath the busy exterior. In this time of reminiscence it is the "little things" that recall Father Becker, such a time perhaps when he would demonstrate for a wondering freshman the gentle art of cigarette rolling, the while he was counting out a loan to tide his visitor over during the stress of some particularly urgent social event. Or probably it is a time we recall when he was walking up and down before the entrance to the Healy building, stopping now and then to speak to his genial way a passing student.

Columns could be filled with the recital of those many incidents in the life of Father Becker that endeared him to

Georgetown's student newspaper of record is *The Hoya*, first published on January 14, 1920. *The Hoya* emerged from an elective journalism class where it was called the *Hilltopper*. *The Hoya's* editorial focus was on-campus events with coverage of national or international events only as they affected the campus. This editorial perspective was derided in the 1960s as institutional and shortsighted and led to the creation in 1969 of a competitor campus newspaper, *The Georgetown Voice*.

Completed at a cost of $2.5 million in 1930, the Medical-Dental Building was constructed at the far northwest corner of campus. Early plans called for the new building to be located on N Street between Thirty-Sixth and Thirty-Seventh Streets. Although this location would have positioned the school adjacent to the original hospital at Thirty-Fifth and N Streets, Pres. W. Coleman Nevils, SJ, felt that future development of the Medical School would be too constrained if located on a neighborhood street.

This 1930 photograph shows a multitude of Ritter equipment in the Dental Infirmary, part of the new Medical-Dental Building. Georgetown's Dental School traced its founding to 1901, when the Washington Dental School was acquired and integrated into Georgetown's Medical School. A decision to close the Dental School—the largest private dental school in the nation at the time—was made in 1987 because of a looming financial disaster and fears that the school's quality would deteriorate as the number of students going into dentistry plummeted nationwide.

This photograph shows the medical library shortly after the Medical-Dental Building opened in 1930. The original Medical School library was founded in 1912 by Dr. George M. Kober, dean of the Medical School. The library's first texts were donated from doctors on the staff and from the personal library of Dr. Kober and US surgeon general Dr. John B. Hamilton.

This Law School class, pictured in 1921, was led by Prof. Charles Keigwin, one of the first faculty members hired for full-time teaching. Although one of the largest law schools at the turn of the 20th century, Georgetown did not follow other leading schools in creating a day program or increasing its admissions standards. In fact, Georgetown withdrew from the Association of American Law Schools in 1905 rather than comply with the association's new standard requiring a high school diploma for admission.

Pictured is the 1938 Law School Annual Banquet. At the time, the Law School was in the midst of rapid change under the leadership of Francis Lucey, SJ, the school's regent for 30 years. The clinical program, which is a hallmark of today's Law Center, was established in 1936, and in the same year, admissions standards were changed to require a four-year college degree, making Georgetown one of only seven law schools with this requirement at the time.

The building at left, decorated with bunting for Georgetown's 150th anniversary in 1939, is the original 1891 portion of the Law School building at 506 E Street. The townhouse seen at the corner was utilized as a dormitory for law students, and the Law Annex Building (far right) was the original home for the SFS. The complex remained in use until 1971, when McDonough Hall was opened.

Pres. W. Coleman Nevils, SJ (1928–1935), was one of the great builders in Georgetown's history. As noted by William McEvitt (C'31, G'32, M'36) in his book *The Hilltop Remembered*, Nevils's "pile drivers and excavators were soon making shambles out of Old Varsity Field and its picturesque grandstand. Here [Nevils] proceeded to erect a 'Greater Georgetown.'" The Greater Georgetown to which McEvitt refers was a revival of an earlier campaign by the same name under John Creeden, SJ, that included plans for the construction of a sports stadium and academic quadrangle.

ANDREW WHITE MEMORIAL QUADRANGLE, GEORGETOWN UNIVERSITY, WASHINGTON, D. C. (UNDER CONSTRUCTION)

This is a rendering of the Andrew White Memorial Quadrangle, the jewel of Coleman Nevils's Greater Georgetown building campaign. Naming buildings in the new quadrangle after Thomas Copley, SJ; John Gravenor, SJ; and Andrew White, SJ, was a deliberate strategy by Nevils to link Georgetown's founding to the arrival of the first Jesuit settlers in Maryland in 1634. Nevils reasoned that the first Jesuit schools in Maryland were the precursors to Georgetown and that the Jesuit educational mission in America continued uninterrupted from St. Mary's City (1634) to Calverton Manor (1640), to Newtown Manor (1677), to Bohemia Manor (1745), and then to Georgetown (1789). In support of his reasoning, Nevils promoted Founders' Day on campus to commemorate the May 25, 1634, landing of Georgetown's "founders" in 1634. Nevils further proclaimed Georgetown, dating to 1634, as the first institution of higher learning in the United States, predating Harvard University by two years.

This 1927 aerial photograph was taken shortly before Coleman Nevils, SJ, became president. The campus would soon be transformed by Nevils's Greater Georgetown building campaign, which in 1930 erected the Medical-Dental Building and relocated athletic fields to the western side of campus.

Plans were drawn up in 1922 under John Creeden, SJ, to erect a 20,000-seat sports stadium near what became the site of the Medical-Dental Building. This drawing anticipated the scope of the project before it was scrapped by Coleman Nevils, SJ, in favor of first building the Andrew White Memorial Quadrangle on the east side of campus to provide dormitory, classroom, and laboratory space. Plans for an on-campus stadium were never realized.

When construction of Copley Hall was commencing in 1929, about 7,000 tons of foundation stones from the demolished M Street bridge crossing Rock Creek were offered to Georgetown for the cost of hauling the stones to campus. The rough-hewn stones, which resembled those used for Healy Hall, were intermixed with tan-colored granite stones from Port Deposit, Maryland, to construct the facades of Copley Hall and the White-Gravenor building.

Copley Hall is named for Thomas Copley, SJ, who is credited with drafting the 1649 Maryland Toleration Act, a law mandating religious tolerance for Trinitarian Christians. The three-story bay window over the central entrance has at its apex a Latin inscription that reads, "Loyola's fortune still may hope to thrive / If men and mould like those of old survive." The seals above the entrance represent the student Sodality, athletics, the Philodemic Society, and the *College Journal*.

Photographed in 1932, stonemasons are completing the facade of the White-Gravenor building. In a 1932 letter to Pres. Herbert Hoover, Coleman Nevils, SJ, explained that the White-Gravenor project would begin early to provide unemployment relief for about 400 men during the nation's "economic emergency."

The White-Gravenor building was erected to house offices for the dean of Georgetown College as well as 20 classrooms, a fireproof vault, and a student cafeteria, Marty's Café, named after the varsity boxing coach. Original plans called for a third building, Poulton Hall, situated to the east of White-Gravenor and across from Copley to form a quadrangle. The economic conditions of the Great Depression made this last structure unaffordable.

Conforming to the Neo-Gothic style of Copley Hall, the White-Gravenor building was completed in 1933. White-Gravenor takes its name from Andrew White, SJ, and John Gravenor, SJ, two of the first Jesuits to come to America with the Lord Baltimore colonists in 1634. The central entrance of the building, like Copley Hall, is a sermon in stone, with each stone ornament having a historical or educational meaning. The stone cross at the top of White-Gravenor's central gable is 10 feet tall and weighs one ton. Below the cross are the seal of Georgetown and the Latin motto of the Society of Jesus, *Ad maiorem Dei gloriam*. The three-story oriel contains symbols of 14 academic fields and the names of Jesuits prominent in those disciplines. Importantly for Coleman Nevils, SJ's, narrative about the history of Georgetown's founding, above the center door are five large carvings that trace the founding of Georgetown University in 1789 to St. Mary's City in 1634.

Students are pictured in 1944 in the senior class reading lounge of Copley Hall. Above the fireplace at left is the mounted head of a buffalo shot in 1872 by Col. William Cody, better known as Buffalo Bill. The trophy was donated to Georgetown by the sister of an alumnus who received it from Civil War Union general Philip Sheridan.

Georgetown professor Chinting Stien is seen in 1942 teaching the Japanese language to Georgetown student-soldiers awaiting their draft into World War II.

In 1943, *The Hoya* ran a headline announcing the admission of women to the graduate school. Pres. Lawrence Gorman, SJ (1942–1949), described the "experimental" action as a "wartime concession." As a result, 11 women enrolled in graduate studies on an equal status with men.

Students relax on Healy Lawn in 1947, with SFS annex buildings visible across Thirty-Seventh Street in the background. Following World War II, 75 percent of students in the SFS were veterans. During the war, the school reorganized its curriculum—adding summer terms and shortening vacations—to allow students to complete a college degree before military indoctrination.

This aerial view of campus is undated, but nearly finished construction of the Walsh Building on East Campus (lower right) and the absence of the Reiss Science Building (adjacent to White-Gravenor) date the photograph to around 1958. The campus saw an aggressive surge in development in the post–World War II years, meeting an urgent need for space but later criticized for lacking an architectural vision. A 1989 master facilities plan commented that the "University has come to realize that some of its past planning decisions and architectural additions have taken place without the benefit of a complete and appropriate master plan."

Edmund Walsh is pictured with Army general Douglas MacArthur during a visit to Japan in 1948. Walsh traveled to Tokyo after serving as a consultant for the International Military Court in Nuremberg, Germany. General MacArthur, who favored the spread of Christianity in postwar Japan, facilitated Walsh's visit, which included an assessment of Jesuit missions in that country.

In 1953, plans were developing for a new building to house the SFS. Early drawings were based on notes by Edmund Walsh, who envisioned an imposing structure jutting out toward the Potomac from a location at the southwest corner of the campus. Walsh's notes describe a statue of Christ high atop the building that would be a national attraction for visitors to Washington, DC.

Financial realities substantially diminished Walsh's ambitions for the SFS building. Designs for the structure were scaled back, and its location was moved to Thirty-Sixth and Prospect Streets. Shown here nearing completion in 1958, the new building, named for Walsh, housed the SFS, the Institute of Languages and Linguistics, and the School of Business Administration until 1982.

This image, dated November 1949, shows students from the Institute of Languages and Linguistics learning to use United Nations–like translation equipment. The institute, opened in October 1949 and housed in a former Sacred Heart school building on Massachusetts Avenue, was a first in US education. Within two years of its founding, the institute offered instruction in 30 languages.

Classes in global business and trade were part of the earliest SFS curriculum, reflecting American views that international commerce was the central concern of the United States in foreign affairs in the 20th century. Highlighting the SFS focus on global commerce, the School of Business Administration, later the McDonough School of Business, was a department in the SFS until it became a separate school in 1957.

The Georgetown Alumni of Greater Miami welcomed Georgetown players and the band to the seventh annual Orange Bowl Classic on January 1, 1941. The Hoyas were depleted by injuries and lost to the unbeaten Mississippi State Maroons 14-7. An estimated 37,000 spectators (a record crowd at the time) attended the game.

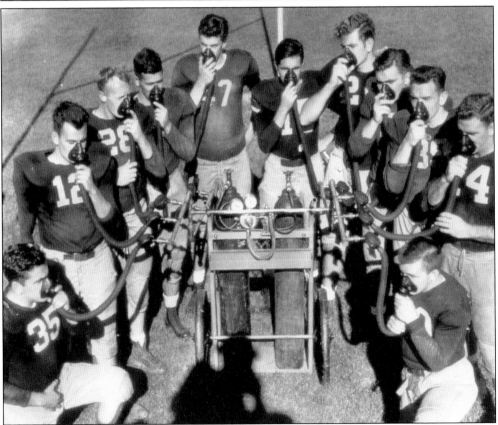

Georgetown football players are photographed in 1946 using an oxygen dispensing go-cart aimed at pepping up weary players. Football was discontinued in 1951 under Pres. Hunter Guthrie, SJ (1949–1952), who felt the sport had "soared completely out of the scale of educational values." Intercollegiate play resumed in 1964.

Alfred C. "Al" Blozis was one of Georgetown's greatest athletes, setting 28 records in football and track and winning the NCAA shot put championship in 1940, 1941, and 1942. Tragically, Blozis died at age 26 fighting in the Vosges Mountains of France in January 1945. An All-America performer in football and track and field, and an All-Pro tackle in the NFL, he was inducted into the National Football Foundation Hall of Fame in 1986 and the USA Track & Field Hall of Fame in 2015.

G. U. Holds Villanova Wildcat Hostage After Kidnap Foray

A signature prank of post–World War II football rivalries was stealing the opposing team's mascot. A letter to the editor of *The Hoya* chronicled the mascot heists of the 1947 season: "We stole the bell from G.W., the Ram (again) from Fordham, made an attempt at Boston's eagle, and finally the snarling monster from Villanova." The November 1947 capture of Villanova University's Count Villain III bobcat made national headlines. William Peter Blatty (C'50), "catnapper" and author of *The Exorcist*, is pictured standing on the left behind the cage. In front of the cage is Georgetown's mascot at the time, a great Dane named Butch. Count Villain III was eventually returned, and Villanova defeated Georgetown 14-12.

Following World War I, boxing became a popular sport on college campuses. Georgetown's boxing team started in 1926 with 70 students, and the school's first intercollegiate boxing match was hosted in 1928 in Ryan Gymnasium against Syracuse University. Intense local rivalries with the University of Maryland and Catholic University fueled interest, and boxing matches routinely drew crowds of 5,000 or more. Changing attitudes about boxing and available funding for the sport led to the dissolution of the varsity team in 1952.

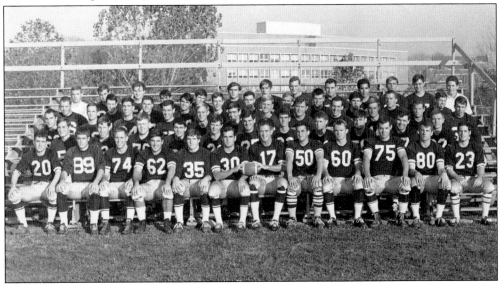

Pictured is the 1966 Georgetown football squad. Patrick McArdle (C'72, L'77) provides context: "The '66 squad was a select team of all-star players from the class intramural football program, which upon the cancellation of intercollegiate varsity football, existed from 1951 through 1966. Intercollegiate football was elevated from club to varsity status at the university in 1970 with eight games scheduled under head coach Scotty Glacken. A Division I institution, Georgetown was permitted by the NCAA in 1973 to classify its football program at the Division III level."

From its founding in 1893, track and field was one of the most popular and successful sports at Georgetown. Track continued through the mid-20th century to be the most nationally prominent sport at Georgetown, according to Emmett Curran. When Frank Gagliano became coach in 1983, Georgetown began a period of success that would include multiple Big East Conference championships, indoor and outdoor titles in IC4A competitions, first place at the Penn Relays, and individual NCAA champions.

A women's athletic association was formed at Georgetown in 1952 and was initially limited to nursing students who played intramural basketball and tennis. The first Georgetown women to win varsity letters were Skippy White (N'57) (far left) and Carol Bloise (N'58) (far right), both of whom competed on the men's sailing team in 1955.

Architects submitted drawings in 1948 for a major expansion of turn-of-the-century Ryan Gymnasium. The sketches depicted the new building as an extension of Ryan, opened in 1906, and fundraising for the project had already begun before the extension plan was scrapped in favor of a free-standing building at the western edge of campus, McDonough Arena.

The ground-breaking ceremony for McDonough Arena took place in 1950. The arena was named for Vincent "Father Mac" McDonough, SJ, director of athletics for 13 years. The new facility provided an on-campus venue for 4,000 fans at basketball games, served as a convocation center and a concert hall, and hosted one of Pres. Dwight Eisenhower's 1953 inaugural balls. This photograph is also notable for the perspective it provides of the vestiges of the campus walks that were later eliminated for mid-campus building projects.

SAMUEL A. HALSEY
PLYMOUTH, N. C.

Samuel A. Halsey Jr. (F'53) was Georgetown's first African American undergraduate alumnus. Halsey was admitted to the SFS two years after Pres. Lawrence Gorman, SJ (1942–1949), urged the deans and regents of Georgetown's schools to admit qualified African American students. No Georgetown school enrolled African American students before 1948, and Georgetown College did not enroll African American students until more than a decade later. In 2002, Georgetown established the Samuel A. Halsey Jr. Citizenship Award to celebrate the accomplishments of notable African American alumni.

This Georgetown Hospital rendering was submitted in 1944 by the architectural firm of Kaiser, Neal, and Reid. The new 400-bed facility received its first patients on July 31, 1947. Since its opening, the hospital and Georgetown University Medical Center research facilities have been greatly expanded with over 60 renovations and additions to maintain its status as a leading research, teaching, and hospital care center.

Looking east from the site of the Medical-Dental Building, this photograph was taken before construction of Georgetown Hospital (1948) and St. Mary's Hall (1956). Visible in the distance to the left is Western High School (now Duke Ellington School of the Arts) as well as homes in the neighborhood of Burleith, built in the 1920s.

The north side of campus was dramatically altered when construction of the hospital began. To the left of the Medical-Dental Building is Georgetown Hospital nearing completion in 1948. St. Mary's Hall was later built as a dormitory for nursing students to the east of the hospital.

Pres. Harry Truman is seen unveiling a dedication plaque in the children's wing of the new hospital building on December 1, 1947. The wing was named in honor of Truman's predecessor, Pres. Franklin Roosevelt. Two years prior, Truman was awarded an honorary degree from Georgetown, the first sitting president to receive such an honor.

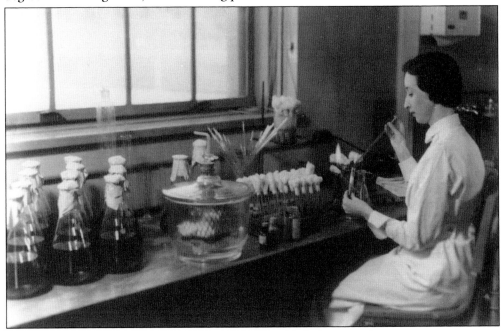

Sarah E. Stewart (M'49), the first female to graduate from the School of Medicine, was a pioneer in the field of viral oncology research. Stewart is credited, along with Dr. Bernice Eddy, with discovering the polyomavirus in 1953 and demonstrating that cancer-causing viruses could be spread from animal to animal. She was nominated for the Nobel Prize for her work.

This photograph shows the early stages of construction for New South dormitory and cafeteria, opened in 1959. Federal funding for higher education research, projects, and buildings increased dramatically in the 1950s. In light of this, Georgetown requested and received federal funding for a new dormitory but was limited to a no-frills building design. The architecture of New South was later critiqued as chunky and banal, with its situation overlooking the Potomac seen by some as broadcasting its design deficiencies to the world.

Edward "Doc" Bunn, SJ (1952–1964), served more than a decade as president and led the "greatest physical expansion in Georgetown history [with a] building program that over fifteen years constructed more buildings than the university had done in its previous 165 years," according to Emmett Curran. Bunn also unified academic and financial administration for the university as well as strategic planning for the main, law, and medical campuses.

The presidency of Gerald Campbell, SJ (1964–1969), was a time of historic changes in the way Georgetown was governed. Under Campbell, the university was incorporated separately from the Society of Jesus, the first laymen were appointed to the board of directors, the Faculty Senate was established, and the University Committee on Rank and Tenure was instituted. In addition, the decision to admit women to Georgetown College was approved. Finally, during Campbell's tenure, the Office of Undergraduate Admissions began recruiting nationally rather than regionally, a strategy that was critical to Georgetown's rise in national rankings for decades to come.

This late 1960s aerial photograph shows the campus transformed by the building campaign of Edward Bunn, much of it related to the expansion of the Medical Center and on-campus housing construction to meet dramatically increased student enrollment. Buildings opened during the Bunn years include St. Mary's, Nevils, Walsh, Kober-Cogan, Gorman, New South, Reiss, Darnall, and Harbin. With this expansion, Georgetown filled pressing functional needs but did so without a clear vision or an architectural plan that complemented the historic campus. As one architectural critic commented in a 1992 report, "The sheer quantity and complexity of construction undertaken during the past 30 years has seriously blurred the clarity of a campus that had grown incrementally but with relatively consistent vision over the previous 170 years." Despite this observation, consistency in architectural planning did not improve as the campus developed. Approved architectural plans were scrapped in light of changing facility needs and availability of funding, leading to campus buildings and spaces that lack coherency and connection.

the G BOOK

1965-66

The norms and conduct of Georgetown gentlemen were outlined in the annual *G Book*. Earlier in the century, the *G Book* outlined specific rules for freshman students, including the directive that freshmen "will wear a distinctive cap everywhere on campus" and "will do any reasonable errand demanded of them by an upper classman." By the 1960s, the book focused on rules prohibiting theft, vandalism, and drinking.

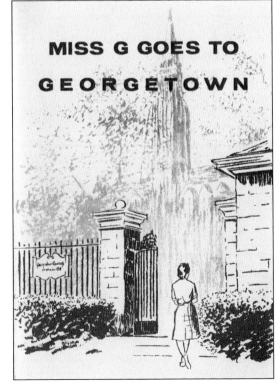

MISS G GOES TO GEORGETOWN

Between 1959 and 1972, a handbook titled *Miss G Goes to Georgetown* was published with guidelines for female students on campus. Women who did not comply with the listed rules were assessed demerits. Infractions included "wearing curlers below the second floor [of the dormitory] (20 demerits)," "dressing without drawing drapes (5 demerits)," and "demonstration of affection anywhere in proximity to the dormitory (50 demerits)." There was no demerit system for male students at the time.

This student was photographed washing the face of the John Carroll statue as part of a hazing ritual in 1946. Other hazing activities included dusting the 175,000 volumes of books in the Riggs Library, polishing the porch of Old North, or walking across campus as a call boy announcing loudly, "Telephone call for John Carroll."

This freshmen versus sophomores pushball game, a freshman hazing event, was photographed during fall 1958. This and other hazing rituals were discontinued in fall 1963 after an alumnus from the class of 1960 brought suit against Georgetown for a disabling injury he sustained during hazing. According to a 1961 *Washington Star* article, the man was injured while "a member of a group of freshmen who were compelled to move around campus in an 'elephant march' to an area where they were to be given a mud bath."

The tradition of having a bulldog serve as Georgetown's mascot dates to 1962, when a student committee led by Stan Samorajczyk (C'64) decided that an English bulldog would best exemplify the tenacious qualities of Georgetown athletes. After the university declined to fund their request for a live mascot, the committee raised funds through dances and selling "stock shares," earning enough money to pay for a two-year-old champion show dog officially named Lil-Nan's Royal Jacket, whose nickname was Jack. The students tried to rename the dog Hoya, but the stubborn bulldog would only answer to Jack. Thereafter, Georgetown's bulldog mascots have always been called Jack.

In 1977, Georgetown began the tradition of using a dog costume in place of an actual bulldog as team mascot at sporting events. Pat Sheehan (C'81), was the first student to play the role.

The Georgetown Chimes were founded in 1946 by Frank Jones (L'48, LLM'52). About the group's name, Jones recalled that "Many a night we would sing under the trees in front of Copley Hall and Healy Hall. As yet, we had no name for the group. One night in 1948 as we were singing, the Healy tower bells rang out at midnight. It was incredibly beautiful. I said to the quartet, 'That's our name, The Georgetown Chimes.' " The Chimes emerged as a Georgetown institution and each year since 1973 has hosted the *Cherry Tree Massacre*, an intercollegiate a cappella performance. In 1962, the Chimes began the tradition of Chimes Night at the Tombs.

The corner of Thirty-Sixth and N Streets is pictured prior to 1962 when Richard McCooey (C'52) opened the Tombs and 1789 restaurant. McCooey modeled the Tombs after Mory's Temple Bar at Yale. The pub's name recalls a line in T.S. Eliot's Old Possum's Book of Practical Cats, in which Bustopher Jones, the Cat About Town, sometimes lunches at "the Tomb."

A REALISTIC APPROACH
TO
STUDENT GOVERNMENT

BILL CLINTON

CANDIDATE

PRESIDENT OF THE STUDENT COUNCIL
MAR. 8 1967

Pres. Bill Clinton (F'68) won earlier student government elections as class leader but lost this prized bid to be president of the East Campus Student Council. About Clinton's early days on campus, *Georgetown* magazine recalled the story of his arrival as a freshman in 1964: Francis P. Dinneen, SJ, professor of linguistics, upon meeting Clinton, asked him "why in the world a Southern Baptist with no foreign languages wanted to come to Georgetown University with intentions of majoring in international relations." Clinton replied, "I've thought about it, and this is where I want to be. In a year we'll see whether I'm right or you are."

Dr. Patricia Rueckel was appointed Georgetown's first dean of women in 1961 when record numbers of women were studying in all of Georgetown's schools except Georgetown College. Rueckel became vice president for student development in 1971, the first woman to be appointed a vice president at a Jesuit university. Rueckel is pictured here dispensing advice to a student from a booth modeled after the *Peanuts* comic strip.

```
                    GEORGETOWN UNIVERSITY
                  SCHOOL OF FOREIGN SERVICE

                      FINAL EXAMINATION

Professor Quigley                              20 May 1965
              DEVELOPMENT OF CIVILIZATION II

1.  You may keep this sheet, but do not write on it.
2.  Put your section and roll-number on upper-right corner of exam
    book.
3.  Think out and outline your answer before you begin to write

QUESTION I
        Were the barbarian invasions a cause or a result of the fall of
        Rome?

QUESTION II
        How did the medieval kings build up their royal power?

QUESTION III
        "The late Middle Ages was a period of retrogression." Discuss.
```

In May 1965, Prof. Carroll Quigley, a legendary instructor who began teaching at Georgetown in 1941, posed three final-exam questions to students in his Development of Civilization II class. Quigley's concept of "future preference"—sacrificing in the present for future need—was cited by former student Bill Clinton in his speech accepting the Democratic nomination for president in 1992.

The Black Student Alliance (BSA) was created in 1968 and led by Bernard White (C'69), who was also the first African American to play for Georgetown's basketball team. According to the club's constitution, the BSA was formed for the purpose of "re-instilling in ourselves that pride which has systematically been driven out of our ancestors and of educating both ourselves and members of the Georgetown University community." The BSA successfully lobbied for the creation in 1970 of a gathering space called The Black House, originally located at 3619 O Street NW.

Richard McSorley, SJ, founder of the Center for Peace Studies at Georgetown, demonstrated in 1971 against the presence of the US Army Reserve Officers Training Corps (ROTC) on campus. Advocating nonviolent solutions to world problems, McSorley had a long arrest record for protests. So popular were his classes in peace studies that students would overflow the classroom and often take the course for no credit.

Five

TOWARD A THIRD CENTURY

Historic changes across American culture, the Catholic Church, and higher education during the late 1950s and 1960s set the stage for the presidency of Timothy S. Healy, SJ, and the advent of Georgetown's third century. One hundred years prior, Patrick Healy set forth an audacious vision and vaulted Georgetown forward. This time, another (unrelated) Healy would lead the transformation.

Healy's presidency benefited from the remarkable contributions of the three presidents who immediately preceded him: Edward Bunn's expansion of campus facilities and administrative consolidation; Gerald Campbell's changes in university governance to include laypeople, as well as the admission of women to Georgetown College; and Robert Henle's reversal of the deteriorating financial situation, placing Georgetown on firm financial footing for the first time in almost a decade.

There were noteworthy physical changes on campus in the late 1960s and 1970s. Lauinger Library opened on the main campus, and Bernard McDonough Hall opened on the Law Center campus. More significant changes took place in campus culture, including a dramatic increase in the number of women and minorities as students, protests for social justice, and calls for an end to the Vietnam War. The climate of dissent of Georgetown students inspired the creation of an independent corporation, Students of Georgetown Inc., with legal standing to sue the university, if necessary, to contest university decisions or policies.

The wave of changes continued in the 1980s as Healy implemented a strategy that, by the time of the school's bicentennial, positioned Georgetown in the top ranks of national research universities with an endowment that had grown fivefold in a decade. It is doubtful that John Carroll would recognize the school he founded 200 years prior, but Georgetown in 1989 very certainly exceeded his expectations.

The Hoya

Vol. LI, No. 21   GEORGETOWN UNIVERSITY, WASHINGTON, D.C.

College May Admit Girls; Student Opinions Sought

Coeds might well be admitted to the all-male College of Arts and Sciences come September of 1969. The College's faculty has informally agreed to the proposal, but students and alumni are yet to be consulted. If reaction is favorable, a study will be conducted during the summer to ascertain the effect of an increased College enrollment on classroom and dormitory space and student-ward it to the University Board of Directors.

According to the Rev. Thomas R. Fitzgerald, S.J., academic vice president, "a reasonable amount, not just a handful" of girls would be admitted to the Class of '73, perhaps 50 to 100. He noted that discussion is being taken up at this point so that the admissions office would have ample time in which to process applications. Fr.

luding February's tuition increase controversy, he remarked, "In no sense are we going to say, 'This is what we've done.'" He added "We will also have the alumni to cope with."

The Rev. Royden B. Davis, S.J., College dean, indicated that he and Fr. Fitzgerald had discussed the possibility of College coeds for some time. Fr. Davis brought up the question to his executive

On May 2, 1968, *The Hoya* carried news that Georgetown would enroll women in Georgetown College for the first time, starting in the fall of 1969. The decision broke a 179-year-old practice of males only in the College. That year, the admissions office was flooded with over 500 applications for only 50 spots allocated to women.

Women have studied at Georgetown continuously since the founding of the Training School for Nurses in 1903. But not until a 1968 board of directors' decision did Georgetown College make the transition to co-education. Marla Angermeier was officially the first woman admitted to the College. She graduated in 1972.

The first issue of *The Georgetown Voice* appeared on March 1, 1969. The *Voice* was created to counter *The Hoya's* perceived conservative editorial voice and its policy to report about only campus news and events. The inaugural editorial of the *Voice* took aim at its competitor: "We shall not limit our editorial content to campus topics. There are more important matters to be discussed than parietals and the fate of the 1789 [restaurant]." Editors of *The Hoya* proposed a merger with the *Voice* in 1970, a proposal that *Voice* editors rejected.

This photograph was taken on May 3, 1971, as Washington, DC, police fired tear gas outside Lauinger Library to disperse protesters who had descended onto campus to seek shelter during the May Day disturbances. Days later, students protesting the university's response occupied the hallway outside the president's office in Healy Hall and were suspended by Pres. Robert Henle, SJ (1969-1976), when they refused to leave.

This photograph, taken in 1969, shows Lauinger Library under construction. Dedicated in 1970 and built at a cost of $6.6 million, the facility was named for Joseph Mark Lauinger, a 1967 alumnus killed in the Vietnam War.

Designed by John Carl Warnecke, the library's modern design was intended to relate Lauinger to its historical context while remaining within a modern and abstract idiom. Lauinger's irregular outline and pronounced vertical emphasis reflect the ornate turrets and decorations of Healy Hall. Lauinger's exposed granite chip concrete façade relates to the dark stonework of Healy. Warnecke was the architect of Village A, built later in the decade and also designed to relate to existing campus architecture.

Edmund G. Ryan, SJ, vice president for educational affairs under Robert Henle, joined students in the February 1973 "Lemonstration" that dumped 3,000 fresh lemons outside the president's office. Students were protesting a recently announced tuition increase, an on-campus housing shortage, and what was described as the deteriorating quality of education at Georgetown. Ryan was later fired by Henle without public explanation, sparking a series of student protests.

In the style of a war protest, students seeking an explanation for the 1974 termination of Edmund Ryan gathered in the Quad for a candlelight vigil. A sign at bottom right reads, "Free Fast Eddie."

The filming of the 1973 movie *The Exorcist* took place on campus in the fall of 1972. The film's producer, William Peter Blatty (C'50), based his story on the actual exorcism of a 14-year-old boy from Mount Rainier, Maryland. The boy, whom Blatty disguised in his novel as 12-year-old Regan MacNeil, was reported by the *Washington Post* on August 19, 1949, to have been treated at Georgetown Hospital during and after the exorcism ritual, which was conducted between 20 and 30 times over a two-month period in Washington, DC, and St. Louis, Missouri.

Pres. Timothy S. Healy, SJ (1976–1989), appears in this 1982 commencement photograph with honorary degree recipient St. Teresa of Calcutta. Healy, not related to the 19th-century Patrick Healy, was at the time the longest-serving president in Georgetown's history. During his tenure, student housing complexes Villages A, B, and C were built as well as the Intercultural Center, Yates Field House, the Edward Bennett Williams Law Library, and the Leavey Student Center. Undergraduate admission rates dropped from 44 percent in 1976 to 23 percent in 1989, minority enrollment increased from 6 to 19 percent, and the Hoyas won their first-ever national basketball championship. Moreover, Healy set out to address Georgetown's lack of an adequate endowment. Fundraising campaigns during his tenure raised the endowment fivefold. Healy was also at the center of sharp debate over Georgetown's position as the nation's oldest Catholic university and its relations with the District of Columbia and federal governments.

The 1971 May Day disturbances and related tensions between the university and students gave rise to a movement to create an independent corporation for students that would provide legal standing for students separate from the university. Founded in 1972, Students of Georgetown Inc. (the Corp) created a private, nonprofit business operated entirely by students independent of the university. The Corp evolved into a commercial entity that students used to launch a small food co-op originally located in New South known as Vital Vittles and also gave rise to book and record co-ops and a travel service as well as typewriter and television rentals. The Corp is today the largest entirely student-run corporation in the country.

While students led the call for many years, it took the 1980 accidental death of a student on campus for the university to authorize the creation of a student-led first responder service called the Georgetown Emergency Response Medical Service (GERMS). Students took emergency response certification courses, and in spring 1983, GERMS purchased its first ambulance: a used Chevy Suburban that the students painted blue and white. GERMS is today the largest all-volunteer, student-run university EMS in the country.

In 1973, the Students of Georgetown Inc. initiated a transportation shuttle when an on-campus housing shortage created the need for affordable transportation to and from campus. Building on the shuttle service concept, the university created the Georgetown University Transportation Society (GUTS) in 1974. GUTS was established as a transportation "society" so it could limit ridership to university faculty, students, and staff, and thereby avoid conflict with the existing DC Metrobus transportation "service" (Metrobus). Distinctive Mercedes-Benz GUTS buses employed all-student drivers and ran loops from Healy Circle to Arlington, the Law Center, and Alban Towers.

Frustrated by inconvenient and expensive campus banking services exclusively provided by the on-campus Riggs Bank (teller hours that did not align with student schedules, long lines to cash checks, and a $10 monthly fee to maintain an account), a group of three students secured a federal charter in 1983 for the Georgetown University Student Federal Credit Union (GUSFCU), known today as the Georgetown University Alumni Student Federal Credit Union (GUASFCU). GUASFCU's first office was a maintenance closet in the O'Gara Building (which stood on the present site of Village C). Operations moved to the basement of Healy Hall—at the time, a center of student life—and later to the Leavey Center. GUASFCU is today the largest entirely student-run credit union in the world.

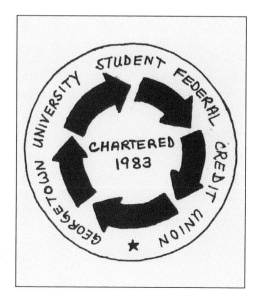

On April 2, 1984, led by coach John Thompson, the Georgetown men's basketball team won the NCAA championship by defeating the University of Houston 84-75, a first-ever NCAA Division I team championship for Georgetown. Writing in the *Washington Post*, reporter John Feinstein quoted Houston star player Ahakeem Olajuwon's praise for the Hoyas: "They do everything a great team should do. They don't care who scores, who takes the shots. That's the difference. They aren't a selfish team. The unselfish team won." The term "Hoya Paranoia" was used by reporters to deride the discipline, intense defensive skills, and physicality of play employed by the championship team under Thompson. Georgetown fans proudly adopted the phrase. (Courtesy of Fred J. Maroon.)

After the Hoya's NCAA victory, a color poster was created by Chris Simms (C'84) depicting the team center, Patrick Ewing (C'85), who was named Most Valuable Player of the tournament. After Georgetown, Ewing had an 18-year NBA career, became a member of the US Olympic Hall of Fame, and was a two-time inductee into the Basketball Hall of Fame.

The Ewing poster appeared around campus, including at the checkout register of The Corp's convenience store, Saxa Sundries, adjacent to Vital Vittles in the basement of Healy Hall. Saxa's, as it was called, sold a wide variety of products including record albums, school supplies, Pepsi products (Vital Vittles sold only Coke products), pantyhose, and film processing.

The 200-foot-tall clock tower of Healy Hall, shown here during a 1983 restoration, is perhaps the most recognizable icon of the Georgetown campus. The tower contains three cast-iron bells installed in 1888. The largest bell is named for the Virgin Mary, Seat of Wisdom. The other two bells are named for patron saints of youth, St. Aloysius Gonzaga, SJ, and St. John Berchmans, SJ. The bells toll on the quarter hour and hourly, and play the "Angelus" at noon and 6:00 p.m. The clock was wound by hand by a Jesuit brother until 1931, when an electric mechanism was installed. Despite the fact that the tower is secure, the clock hands have been stolen many times over the years. A 1980s issue of *The Hoya* provided a detailed description of how to gain access to the tower. Not a harmless prank, stealing the clock hands has left the clock and bells inoperable and in need of expensive repairs.

The Edward B. Bunn, SJ, Intercultural Center opened in 1982, six years after Congress offered grants to support the creation of model intercultural programs to study the cultural basis of international conflict. In response, Georgetown proposed and received funding for an intercultural center that would house the SFS and create new intercultural educational programs. Congress also agreed to fund a non-academic building feature, the world's largest-ever solar roof.

Georgetown opened the Thomas and Dorothy Leavey Student Center in 1988. Designed to reflect the Victorian style of the Quad-facing brick façade of Healy Hall, the Leavey Center was strategically located to mediate between the institutional architecture of the medical complex and the finer textures of the historic campus. Leavey was part of a Tiered Architectural Podia Plan that envisioned several more Leavey-like buildings that would slope downward to the southern edge of campus. The Podia Plan was not implemented beyond the first building, Leavey.

137

Georgetown's Medical Center established a cancer center in 1970 and named it in honor of Vincent T. Lombardi, renowned former coach of the Green Bay Packers and the Washington Redskins, who was treated for cancer at Georgetown University Hospital. A new facility for the Lombardi Comprehensive Cancer Center opened in 1982 to house all oncological diagnosis, research, and treatment activities. Lombardi was designated in 1974 and remains a comprehensive cancer center today. Only 51 of approximately 1,500 cancer centers in the United States are designated as comprehensive cancer centers, and they serve as national leaders in cancer treatment, research, and education.

The Law Center campus was greatly enhanced in 1989 by the addition of the Edward Bennett Williams Law Library. Williams was a 1944 graduate of the Law School and worked for more than four decades as Georgetown's legal counsel. He was renowned as a trial lawyer, defending high profile clients such as Sen. Joseph McCarthy, Jimmy Hoffa, and John Hinckley Jr.

Kennedy Center architect Edward Durell Stone designed McDonough Hall as a new home for the Law Center. (The Law School was renamed the Law Center in 1953 to represent the expanded scope of the school and to signal a more ambitious institution of legal education.) Located at 600 New Jersey Avenue NW, the building's original design, which called for a marble facade, was substantially altered due to cost-cutting (white bricks were used instead). The building was named for Bernard P. McDonough, a 1925 graduate of the Law School; his $1 million gift was the largest ever received by the university at the time.

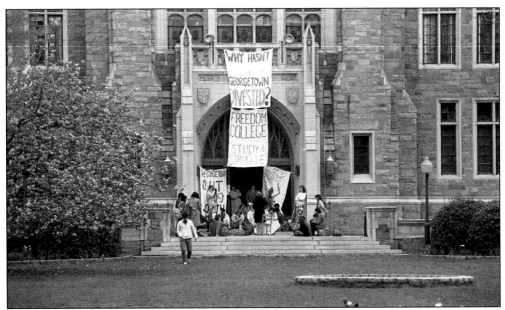

The Student Coalition against Racism (GU-SCAR) organized a teach-in called Freedom College in April 1986 to protest and raise awareness about the university's investment in companies that did business in Apartheid South Africa. Thirty-five student protesters were arrested for erecting a shanty on Copley Lawn as part of the protest. The university Board of Directors voted in fall 1986 to divest all its holdings in 45 companies that did business in South Africa, 16 percent of the school's endowment at the time.

After seven years of litigation, the District of Columbia Court of Appeals ruled in November 1987 that two student groups, the Gay People of Georgetown University and the Gay Rights Coalition of the Georgetown University Law Center, must receive equal access to university facilities and services. As part of the ruling, the court upheld Georgetown's right to withhold "official recognition" from the group on religious grounds. The university immediately filed a stay with the Supreme Court but was denied. Finally, the Board of Directors voted in March 1988 to accept the ruling of the Appeals Court. Timothy Healy, SJ, wrote to a divided and skeptical university community, "the [Court] addressed what the university always felt to be the principal issue in the case, its right to adhere to its religious heritage." The logo pictured was created after Georgetown, in 2008, become the first Catholic university in the nation to establish and fund a fulltime LGBTQ resource center.

The tradition of hosting commencement and other important academic events on Healy Lawn dates to 1902. Pictured is an unusual photographic perspective of the audience that gathered for the bicentennial convocation when Pres. Ronald Reagan was awarded an honorary degree. Reagan was introduced by Georgetown professor Jeane Kirkpatrick, whom Reagan appointed as US permanent representative to the United Nations, the first woman to hold that post.

A bicentennial logo derived from the university seal was created to celebrate Georgetown's 200th year. At the center of the seal is an oak branch, signifying strength, crossed by a laurel branch, signifying peace and victory. Both are pointed to Georgetown's founding year and its bicentennial year. Framing the shield are the words Learning, Faith, and Freedom, representing Georgetown's missions and ideals.

Alumnus Robert Collier wrote the "Alma Mater" as a student in 1894. The song originally began with the words, "Sons of Georgetown, Alma Mater." In 1981, after a campaign led by Carol Hession Powers (N'41), the opening words were changed and a later line, "We're Georgetown sons forever" was replaced with "May Georgetown live forever."

Hail, oh Georgetown, Alma Mater,
Swift Potomac's lovely daughter,
Ever watching by the water,
Smiles on us today.

Now her children gather 'round her,
Lo, with garlands they have crowned her,
Reverent hands and fond enwound her,
With the Blue and Gray.

Wave her colors ever,
Furl her standards never,
But raise it high,
And proudly cry,
May Georgetown live forever.

Where Potomac's tide is streaming,
From her spires and steeples beaming,
See the grand old banner gleaming:
Georgetown's Blue and Gray.

(Photograph by Phil Humnicky.)

BIBLIOGRAPHY

Ballman, Francis X. *Building Outlines Campus Buildings, 1789–1995*. Washington, DC: Georgetown University Archives, unpublished manuscript, 1995.

Curran, Robert Emmett. *A History of Georgetown University*. Washington, DC: Georgetown University Press, 2010.

Daley, John M., SJ. *Georgetown University: Origin and Early Years*. Washington, DC: Georgetown University Press, 1957.

Durkin, SJ, Joseph T., ed. *Swift Potomac's Lovely Daughter: Two Centuries at Georgetown through Student's Eyes*. Washington, DC: Georgetown University Press, 1990.

———. *Georgetown University: First in the Nation's Capital*. Garden City, NY: Doubleday & Company, 1964.

Easby-Smith, James S. *Georgetown University in the District of Columbia, 1789–1907, Its Founders, Benefactors, Officers, Instructors and Alumni*. New York, Chicago: The Lewis Publishing Company, 1907.

Mitchell, Mary. *Divided Town: A Study of Georgetown, D.C. During the Civil War*. Barre, MA: Barre Publishers, 1968.

McEvitt, William G. *The Hilltop Remembered*. Washington, D.C.: Georgetown University Library, 1982.

Reynolds, Jon K. and Barringer, George M. *Georgetown University, A Pictorial Review*. Baltimore, MD: The Charles B. DeVilbiss Company, 1976.

Rooney, Francis. *The Global Vatican: an inside look at the Catholic church, world politics, and the extraordinary relationship between the United States and the Holy See*. Lanham, MD: Rowman & Littlefield, 2013.

Shea, John Gilmary, SJ. *History of Georgetown University in the District of Columbia*. New York, NY: P.F. Collier, 1891.

Tillman, Seth P. *Georgetown's School of Foreign Service: The First 75 Years*. Washington, DC: Georgetown University Press, 1994.

Warner, William A. *At Peace with All Their Neighbors: Catholics and Catholicism in the National Capital 1787–1860*. Washington, DC: Georgetown University Press, 1994.

DISCOVER THOUSANDS OF LOCAL HISTORY BOOKS FEATURING MILLIONS OF VINTAGE IMAGES

Arcadia Publishing, the leading local history publisher in the United States, is committed to making history accessible and meaningful through publishing books that celebrate and preserve the heritage of America's people and places.

Find more books like this at
www.arcadiapublishing.com

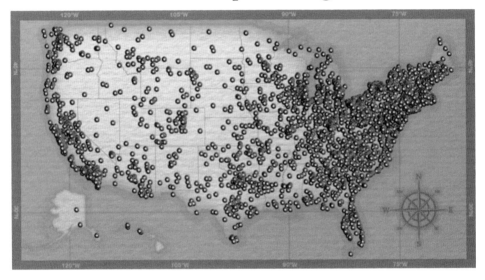

Search for your hometown history, your old stomping grounds, and even your favorite sports team.